fabulous FASHION DOLL CLOTHING you can make

fabulous

FASHION
DOLL CLOTHING

you can make

No Sewing Required

Tina Casey

NORTH LIGHT BOOKS
Cincinnati, Ohio

About the Author

Tina Casey grew up in Pittsburgh, Pennsylvania. She learned how to sew from her mother, sister and the upstairs lodger. Ms. Casey started sewing professionally while still a teenager, embroidering clothes with beads and reproducing vintage fashions.

Ms. Casey moved to New York City in 1980 and worked her way through college as a sample hand for a top independent fashion designer. Upon graduation, she entered the white-collar field and sewing became her avocation. In addition to doll clothes, she has applied herself to hand-pieced and machine-pieced quilts, backpacks, hats, shoes, handbags, wedding gowns, toys, drapery, upholstery and tailored suits. She is heavily involved with beads and has also been known to knit.

This is Ms. Casey's second book. Her first, *Creating Extraordinary Beads From Ordinary Materials*, is also published by North Light Books.

Fabulous Fashion Doll Clothing You Can Make. Copyright © 1999 by Tina Casey. Manufactured in China. All rights reserved. No part of this book may be reproduced in any form or by any electronic or mechanical means including information storage and retrieval systems without permission in writing from the publisher, except by a reviewer, who may quote brief passages in a review. Published by North Light Books, an imprint of F&W Publications, Inc., 1507 Dana Avenue, Cincinnati, Ohio 45207. (800) 289-0963.

First edition.

Other fine North Light Books are available from your local bookstore, art supply store or direct from the publisher.

03 02 01 00 99   5 4 3 2 1

Library of Congress Cataloging-in-Publication Data

Casey, Tina

    Fabulous fashion doll clothing you can make / Tina Casey. — 1st ed.

        p.   cm.

    Includes index.

    ISBN 0-89134-890-5 (pbk. : alk. paper)

    1. Doll clothes—Patterns.   I. Title.

TT175.7.C39 1999   98-40868

745.592'2—dc21   CIP

Editor: Joyce Dolan

Production editor: Marilyn Daiker

Designer: Mary Barnes Clark

Production Coordinator: John Peavler

Cover photograph by Pamela Monfort Braun

To Paula, Henry, Amy and David, who
put up with me all these years. Then
again, they didn't have a choice.

To Neil, Marie, Barbara, Tom and
Sharon, because in-laws don't get
to choose, either.

To Monica, although I suspect the
only reason that she puts up with me
is because I put up with her.

And especially to Eddie, who took
a chance on being able to put up with
me forever. I would also like to thank
Tommy and Paulina for assisting
him in this endeavor.

Table of Contents

I *had the card, the guts and a doll in desperate need. I grew up in one of those do-it-yourself families and, while we were not expected to make our own dolls, it was assumed that we would take responsibility for furnishing their wardrobes.*

Unfortunately, no matter how many books I read, I didn't get it. I couldn't sew a stitch to save my life. My doll spent her best years draped in a kind of primitive serape made from a dust cloth, which I justified with the explanation that her significant other was a vagabond troll and she was dressing down to show solidarity.

By the time I learned how to sew, I had a life. It did not include dolls. Then I had a kid, plenty of dolls and no time to sew anything for any of them. All of my friends were in the same fix. A cloud of guilt hung over the playground. Our childhoods had been enriched by a sister, a mother, someone who made doll clothes for us—and our own children were getting zippo.

Then one day my friend Monica revealed how a fabulous gown could be had for the price of a sock and thirty seconds of free time. It was the answer to all of our problems. All it needed was a little fine-tuning. . . .

This book is the result of several years of fine-tuning. There is no sewing in this book. There is no pressing. There are no patterns. There is no setting in of sleeves, turning of collars, rolling of lapels or tearing out of hair. Just glamour and more glamour.

Enjoy!

1 Tools & Materials

If you don't know how to sew, if you don't have time to sew, or if you believe sewing is a nefarious plot hatched by superior beings from another planet bent on conquering the Earth, you can still make fabulous doll clothes. The idea is to get somebody else to do most of the work for you.

Somebody else, as defined in this book, means anyone who manufactures socks, ties, scarves, napkins, doilies, and other ready-made items that one does not usually associate with doll clothes. They give you a running start. They practically turn themselves into runway-quality ensembles before you can say, "I'll take that in a size 8." In fact, most of the things in this book have probably been in your closet for years, just waiting for the chance to prove themselves. Put them on a doll, snip off the parts that don't fit, and glue the ragged edges. Now your sock is a fashion hero.

Materials

You can make runway-quality fashion statements from socks…

From sock to hero.

…neckties…

…napkins, washcloths, doilies…

…scarves…

...craft shop findings or even findings from the bottom of your kitchen drawer.

Dress up hats and accessories with strings of sequins and pearls, buttons, plastic beads or miniature flowers and gilt berries.

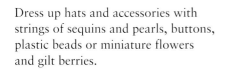

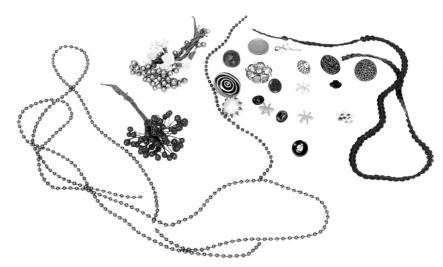

Add extra snap to a basic outfit with funky stuff like fringe, rickrack, lace, sequins, or feather parts. An old blouse is a good source for jazzy scraps of fabric, like the gold and pink shown here.

The Dolls

The fashions in this book can fit dolls of various sizes. I've used fashion dolls as my fitting models. A fashion doll is approximately 11½" (29.2cm) of undiluted glamour with the kind of figure that sends the imagination into flights of fancy. Since my designs do not employ premeasured pattern pieces, it's easy to adapt them for shorter dolls, taller dolls and dolls of more earthbound proportions.

The fashions in this book can be adapted for a range of sizes and body types.

Fashion dolls are made by many different toy companies, but they all share the same basic proportions: approximately 11½" (29.2cm) tall with long legs, a small waist and enthusiastic chest.

Protect the doll's hair from glue. Before you get to work, consider the effect of glue on your model. You might want to protect her hair, perhaps with a plastic bonnet. You can also use plastic wrap to protect the doll's skin from glue or fabric paint.

The fashion dolls in this book were picked up on Delancy Street in lower Manhattan. While cheaply priced, they share the same basic proportions as their more expensive uptown girl-friends. There are small variations that make a difference if you are designing clothes that fit tightly. Some dolls have bigger hands and feet, some have slimmer arms, some are slightly taller or are more pronounced as to their chest-waist-hip ratio. Head sizes and hairdos also differ from one doll to the next. If you make tightly fitted clothes for a friend's doll, avoid last minute embarrassment—use the same type of doll for your model.

Tools and Notions

Scissors

Utility scissors or small embroidery scissors are fine as long as they are sharp. If you need to buy scissors, get good-quality fabric shears.

Pins, Ruler, Tape

A few pins come in handy, as does a small ruler or measuring tape, but these aren't essential.

Glue

Some outfits can be thrown together without glue, but, generally speaking, you need a fast-bonding craft or fabric glue.

Instead of doing a definitive analysis of the dozens of glues available to craftspeople, I will put it simply: If the glue works, use it. You need a fast-bonding glue, so read the labels and experiment until you find one that works best for you.

Some bottled glues, like the one pictured here, are made with a mild formula and you can handle them with your fingers. Others have some kind of stuff that takes off nail polish. Avoid that by covering your finger in plastic wrap, wearing surgical gloves or by using a small implement like a butter knife to press things together.

Glue Gun

My personal recommendation for gluing: a mini hot-melt glue gun. I was not a glue-gun person until I tried it. Then it became my new best friend. Mini glue guns are cheap and easy to use. The glue bonds fast on all kinds of materials and doesn't give off that pesky chemical smell. It cools down enough to touch within a few seconds of application. It doesn't stick to your fingers and won't take off your nail polish, either.

Initially I declined to try a low-temperature glue gun because the label implied it wouldn't bond quickly enough for my purposes, but eventually I succumbed. It worked just as nicely as the hot-

melt variety. The lesson is that labels are important, but so is personal experience.

Scissors and a glue gun, or a fast-bonding bottled glue, are musts.

Velcro

Velcro was another bête noire of mine, but it's the only way to go to avoid sewing on fasteners. There are hammer-on buttons and snaps, but the ones generally available are too big for fashion doll clothes. Look for self-stick Velcro on the notions rack of any craft or fabric store. True to its name, self-stick Velcro sticks by itself. Trim it down to the size and shape you need, peel off the backing and press it on.

Odds and Ends

Many of my hats are secured on the doll's head by a piece of pipe cleaner or a twist-tie glued inside. I also use loops of elastic or ribbon.

Self-stick Velcro, pipe cleaners, twist-ties, elastic and ribbon are for holding things together. Fabric paint is good for decorating, and also for disguising mistakes. It's also useful for keeping raw edges from fraying. Nail polish can substitute for fabric paint.

2 Witty Knitties

If you would allow me to detail all of the reasons why socks make the greatest doll clothes, you'd be in for a long night. So I'll try to keep it short. The knit fabric gives you the best fit with the least amount of fuss. Trendy clothing stores carry armloads of socks that go with the latest hot looks, so your doll can follow up-to-the-minute fashion. And one sock is good for a dress with matching hat, shoes and bag. If only life were that simple.

Socks

Any sock can be turned into doll clothes, but there is an Ideal Sock. The pink sock pictured here is Ideal. It's the sock that sets off the biggest fashion bang for the least amount of work. Look for a sock that has a cuff decorated with lace, ribbon or some other extra frill. The leg part should be about 2" (5.1cm) across (or a little less than the doll's width from shoulder to shoulder) and about 4" (10.2cm) long with the cuff turned down. That's long enough for a fashion doll minidress. A child's size 4x to 6x sock fits the bill, but since everyone knows that the system for sizing children's socks is confusing it's best to bring the doll along when shopping and check the sock's length and width against her figure.

The other socks pictured here are less than Ideal—too big, too small, too plain—but if you skim through this chapter, you'll see that every sock is a world of marvelousness unto itself, and perhaps needs just a little extra push for it to blossom forth in all its glory.

To see if your sock is the right size, fold down the cuff and place it next to the doll level with her shoulder line. The leg part of the sock should be at least long enough to reach her thigh.

Spring Fling
Spring Fling Dress

You can make a quickie version of the Spring Fling dress with a pair of scissors and about thirty seconds of free time. To give the dress a more polished look and to make the accessories, you'll need glue, a bit of lace and some miniature flowers, buttons or other little decorations.

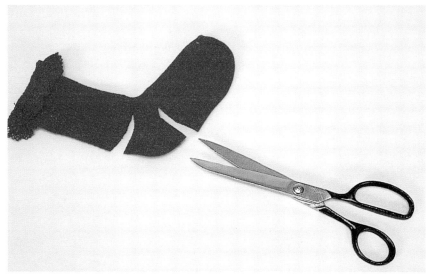

1 Cut the leg part of the sock entirely away from the heel, and cut the heel away from the rest of the foot. As shown, leave a ³/₄" (1.9cm) wide strip extending from the heel. This piece will be used for hats and bags.

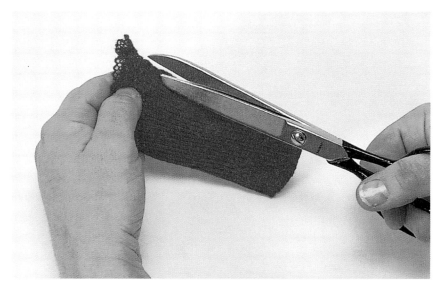

2 Snip a little slit, no more than ¹/₂" (1.3cm) long, in each side of the sock just under the cuff seam. These are the armholes.

"I'll just cut up these old drapes and—what a waste of perfectly good drapes. Why don't I just use this little bitty ol' sock? Clark will be so impressed by my thrifty ways."

Gone With the Wind

3 It's easiest to put the sock on the doll by having her "step" in through the neck opening. If the armholes are too small, snip a little more. Then roll down the collar and this "quickie" version of the dress is complete.

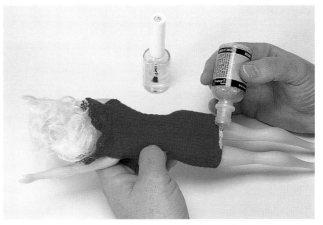

4 To keep the hem from unraveling, dab fabric paint or nail polish around it...

...or fold the hem up and glue it...

...or glue on a bit of lace.

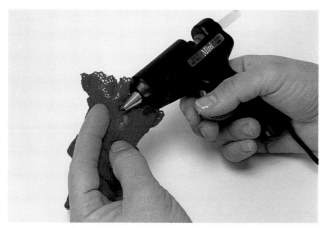

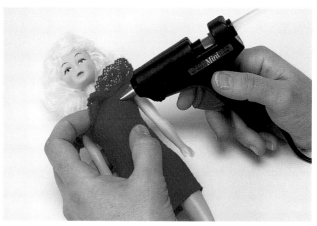

5 The armholes can be treated the same as the hem. Line them with fabric paint or nail polish, or push the edges inside and glue them as shown here.

6 Glue down the collar if it won't stay in place.

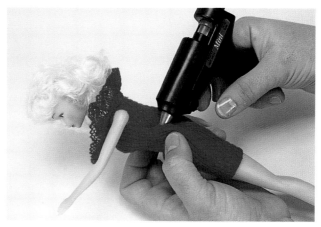

7 To tailor the waist, make a slit in each side of the dress. The slits should be about 1" (2.5cm) long and centered at the waistline.

Then pull the front of the slit over the rear and glue it down behind the doll's back.

Here is the fully tailored minidress with the collar glued down and the waist fitted. The flared skirt was achieved by stretching the hem while gluing it.

Spring Fling Hat

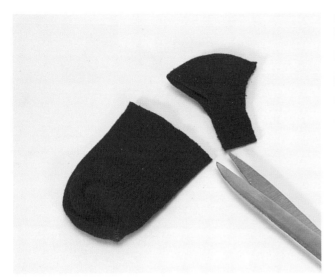

1 Use the heel of the sock. As shown, cut the heel away from the rest of the foot, leaving a ³/₄" (1.9cm) wide strip extending from it.

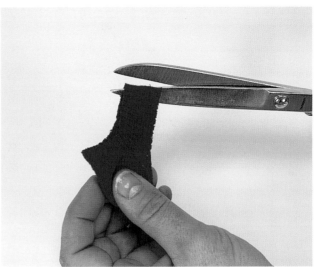

2 Snip open the end of the strip. This completes a quickie version of the hat. Tie it on the doll's head like a kerchief.

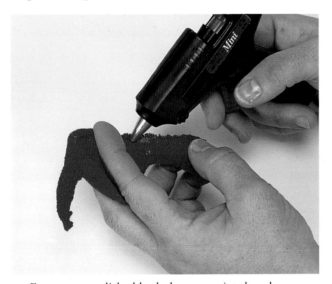

3 For a more polished look, hem or paint the edges all around.

4 Glue a bit of lace to the front along with a flower or fancy button. I snipped the flower off of its stem, keeping only its plastic center.

Spring Fling Tote

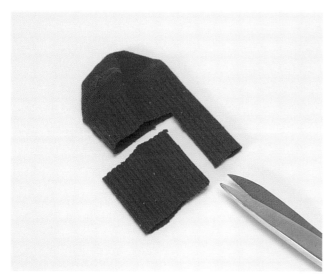

1 Cut a fat "L" shape out of the foot, leaving the toe about 2" (5.1cm) deep, with a strip alongside about 1¹/₂" (3.8cm) long and 1" (2.5cm) wide.

2 Hem all around the edges, including the strip...

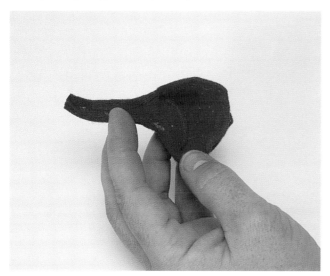

...so that it looks like this.

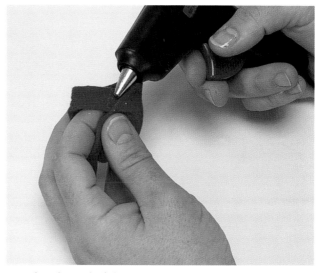

3 Glue the end of the strip to the opposite side. That makes the handle.

Spring Fling Moccasins

1 Cut a rectangle of fabric about 1¹/₂" (3.8cm) wide by 1³/₄" (4.5cm) long. Fold over one end about ¹/₂" (1.3cm) and glue it down thoroughly.

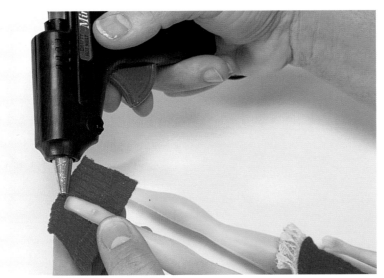

2 Work with the doll facedown. Place the rectangle on her foot, so the unhemmed edge extends just beyond her toes. Put a dot of glue in the middle of that extension.

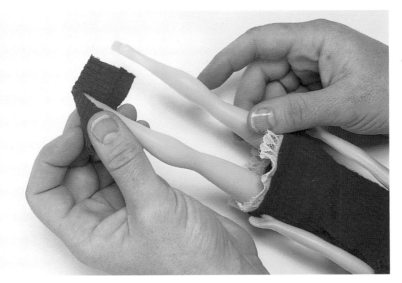

3 Fold one corner of the fabric over the doll's foot, just as if you were making a paper airplane. A dot of glue will hold the tip of the fold in place.

4 Put another dot of glue on the extension....

...Then fold the other corner down. The two sides should overlap in the middle of the doll's foot. If there's much excess, trim it. Push any loose yarns onto the bottom of the moccasin where they won't show. Then glue the overlap down the middle.

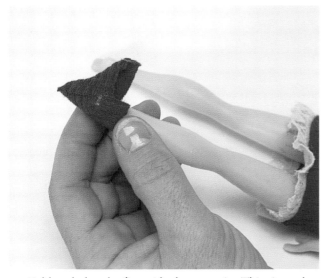

5 Fold and glue the first side down again. This time, the tip of the fold is at the ball of the foot. The stretchy knit allows you to pull the fabric over the heel and up behind the ankle.

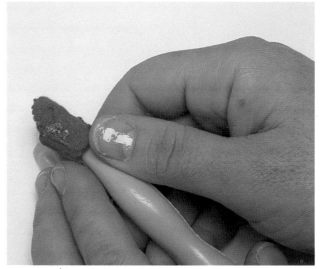

6 Fold and glue the second side the same way. The two sides should overlap down the middle of the foot under the heel and up behind the ankle. If there is excess, trim it off before gluing.

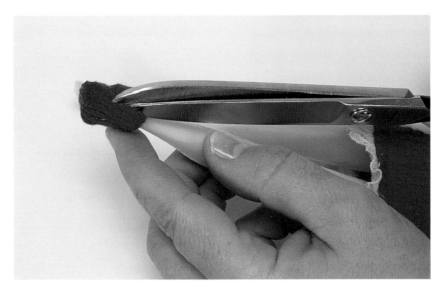

7 For the turned-down cuff, slit the top of the foot down the middle. The slit should go a little less than ¹/₂" (1.3cm) from the edge of the cuff. The extra glue you applied in Step 1 will prevent the edges of the slit from fraying.

8 Fold down the corners of the slit and hold them in place with a dot of glue.

If you can make a paper airplane, you can make a moccasin. It's a rectangle of fabric with the corners folded around the doll's foot. My moccasins always end up with some glue showing on the bottom. It's hard to be neat when the work is so small. You can disguise any mishaps by coating the entire bottom with glue to make a stiff, shiny sole, or by painting over it with fabric paint.

April Showers

Baby socks are too short for fashion doll dresses, but you can easily lengthen them with a piece of eyelet lace. The lace pictured here is 1¹⁄₂" (3.8cm) wide, with all of the little eyes concentrated at the bottom edge where they reveal nothing of consequence.

If the tote bag looks familiar, refer to the Spring Fling hat. Both are made from the heel of the sock along with an extension strip. The difference is that the tote omits Step 2. Leave the heel and its extension intact, and just hem it all around.

April Showers Hat

1 **Top:** For the crown, cut a rectangle of fabric about 3" (7.6cm) wide, and long enough to fit around the doll's head with a slight overlap. Hem the long edges of the rectangle and glue it in a tube.

Bottom: For the brim, use lace about 12" (30.5cm) long—this one is 1¹⁄₄" (3.2cm) wide—and glue pleats in the top edge. When the pleated lace fits around the crown, trim the excess and glue the ends together.

"When Gene asked me out, naturally I assumed that water would be involved."

Singing in the Rain

2 Put glue around the inner edge of the brim and press the crown over it.

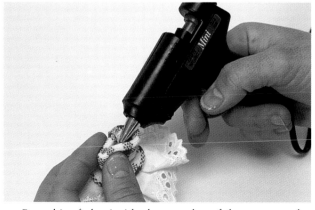

3 Put a bit of glue inside the top edge of the crown and pinch it shut. I also glued down the corners to make a pointed crown.

Summer Style

Socks too small for a dress can make a skirt and top set. Use a pair of baby or toddler socks for this outfit.

The top is similar to the Spring Fling dress. It's made with the sock upside down. The cuff is at the waist. The neckline is hemmed with glue. You can also glue lace around it like the hem of the Spring Fling dress.

To tailor the top, slit the back and put it on the doll. Reglue the back seam so the cuff fits snugly around the waist. Keep the neckline big enough to fit over the doll's head or hips. With glue, paint or lace around it, the neckline won't stretch very much.

Summer-Style Skirt

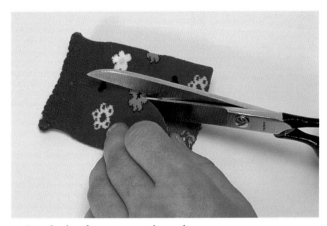

1 Cut the leg from one sock, and slit it all the way open.

"Bruce didn't like me going on the island. What's to worry about? I love monkeys. They're cute."
King Kong

2 Put the sock on the doll and fit it snugly around the waist and hips. Trim the excess and glue the seam from top to bottom.

Summer-Style Hairband

Cut a ³/₄" (1.9cm) wide strip of sock long enough to fit around the doll's head with a slight overlap. Hem each long side of the strip, then glue the ends together to form a loop. Glue on a small flower or button.

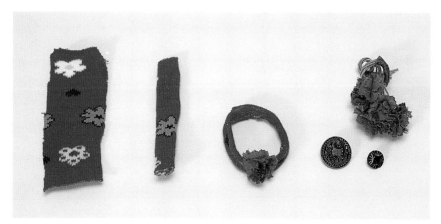

Summer-Style Booties

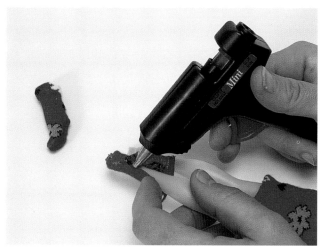

1 Follow the same instructions given for the Spring Fling moccasins. For Step 6, glue the two sides together behind the ankle. Check the fit and trim the excess if necessary. Then continue gluing up the back of the leg.

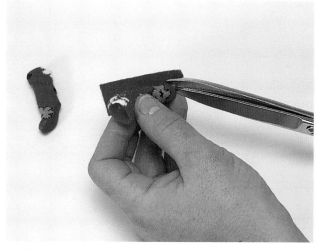

2 To make the sole, glue a scrap of felt or leather on the bottom of the bootie and trim it into shape around the edges.

Like the moccasins, the booties are made from a rectangle of fabric folded over the doll's foot. The bootie rectangle can be a little longer. The bootie is not slit open in front, so it doesn't require a wide hem.

July Jaunt

This two-piece outfit can be made from a single, long sock. The cuffed part is used for the skirt. The remaining part of the leg is used for the top. It's similar to the Summer-Style top, except that both the waistline and the neckline are hemmed.

The moccasins are the Spring Fling moccasins, with a single gilt berry glued at the end of the slit.

Trim the tip of a full-size feather to make a miniature feather like the one in July Jaunt. A small brass stud holds the feather in place. You can find brass studs on the notions rack in many fabric stores. They don't require glue or a special tool. They have four little prongs that you push through the fabric and bend down. I also used them to decorate the shoes.

July Jaunt Hat

"Bogie said he had the bird, so I said I'd bring the stuffing. I think we had a miscommunication there."

The Maltese Falcon

The cap is just the toe of the sock. The toe seam separates the little "brim" from the crown, so when you cut off the toe, cut about ³/₄" (1.9cm) away from the seam. Hem the raw edge all around.

Autumn Intrigue

Besides the usual sock, this outfit uses a bit of fringe. Full-scale fringe overwhelms a fashion doll, so I customized it: it's full length on the hem and hat, trimmed into a V shape for the neckline and cut short for the boots.

The Velcro is optional. It's for attaching a cape to the dress. The black polymer clay is also optional, and is used for making the high-heeled soles for the booties. See chapter five for more information on this wonderful clay.

Materials for Autumn Intrigue

"The invitation said 'Dress for sun and sand.' Peter will have an awful lot of explaining to do when I catch up to him!"

Lawrence of Arabia

Autumn Intrigue Dress

1 Make an April Showers dress. Adjust the neckline so it fits off, not over, the shoulders. This ensures the neck opening will be big enough to go over the doll's head or hips. After the fringe is glued on, it won't be stretchy anymore. Glue fringe all around the neckline and hem.

2 Trim the fringe around the neckline into a V shape.

Autumn Intrigue Hat

This is the Summer-Style hairband with fringe glued all the way around.

Autumn Intrigue Booties

These are Summer-Style booties. Glue fringe around the top, then trim it short. The polymer clay high-heeled soles are described in chapter five.

Autumn Intrigue Cape

Use the other sock leg to make a cape. Glue the top and bottom shut, and add fringe to the bottom. Put Velcro on the upper corners of the cape and behind the doll's shoulders.

November Frost

This is the same outfit as Autumn Intrigue, but with a fur trim instead of fringe. The booties are constructed the same way, but with a rectangle that is long enough to reach midthigh. A doll's midthigh is wider than you may think, so be sure to make the rectangle wide enough to fit around it.

Like fringe, fake fur must be customized to suit the doll's proportions. This fur came ready-cut in a ³/₄" (1.9cm) wide strip. Your local craft or fabric store may carry fur strips in the trimmings aisle. When you only need a small amount, strips are more economical than buying fur fabric by the yard.

I used the full strip for the hat and cape. For the dress hem, I cut the strip in half lengthwise. For the neckline and boot trim, I trimmed the fur short. The armbands are trimmed shorter at the ends and left a bit longer in the middle.

When joining two pieces of fur, trim away all of the fur from the underlapped piece.

"If Ray, Bert and Jack would only stop dancing and keep walking, we'd get home sooner. But—if you can't lick 'em, join 'em."

The Wizard of Oz

November Frost Hat

1 **Left:** To start the crown, cut a circle of fabric about ¹/₂" (1.3cm) bigger than the dolls' head. Cut a pie-shaped piece out of it.

Center: Overlap the edges to form a cone.

Right: The brim is a strip of fur long enough to fit around the doll's head.

2 Push the crown up through the brim from the bottom. Put glue inside the top edge of the brim. If necessary, stretch or pinch the crown to fit the brim.

Winter Follies

Once you've made a sock dress or two, it's just a small side step to sweaters. The sleeve, along with its cuff, can be treated just like a sock. For the Winter Follies dress, I made my own sock: a rectangle of fabric cut from the body of the sweater and glued into a tube.

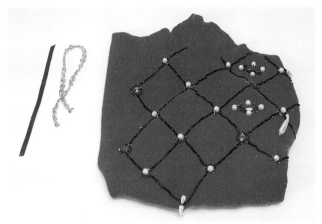

This morning's rummage sale find is tonight's gown. An extra bit of gold trim is optional. The piece of ribbon is for the hat. This sweater is ideal since its bead and pearl embroidery can be clipped off to decorate the dress.

Winter Follies Hat

Left: Cut a small circle from the beaded part of the sweater. (First glue the threads from the inside as described in Step 3 of the dress.) Clip little pie shapes out all around the edge to make a flower shape.
Center: Turn all of the "petals" under, gluing thoroughly.
Right: Glue ribbon or a loop of elastic underneath. The finished hat has gold braid glued around the edge.

"It's not exactly the most sensible thing to wear during tick season, but I want to look good in case Errol swings by."

Robin Hood

Winter Follies Dress

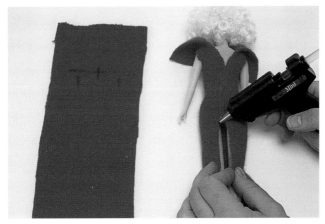

1 **Left:** Cut a rectangle of fabric as long as the doll's height and wide enough to fit around her chest. The rectangle shown here is marked for armholes.

Right: Cut and hem the armholes, then put the rectangle on the doll. Glue the back seam from the shoulder blades to the knees while pulling the fabric snug around the waist.

2 Turn the doll over and trim off the excess fabric from the neckline.

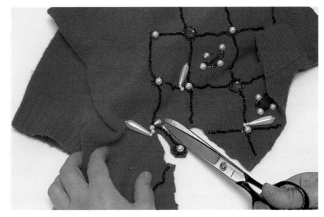

3 Select a section of the beaded fabric. Secure the beads by gluing down the threads from the inside…

…and then cut around the beads. The glue keeps them from coming off.

4 Glue the beads on the neckline. You can also add some extra trim, such as the gold braid shown on the finished dress.

5 To flare the skirt, make a slit from the hem up the front of each leg, ending at the knee. Cut two triangles of fabric about as tall as the slit, and glue one under each slit. Glue a third triangle to the opening left in the back of the dress from Step 1. The finished dress has gold braid glued around the hem.

December Dream

This is the Winter Follies dress made from a plain piece of green sweater. The sweater had no beads and pearls, so I used an elaborate scalloped lace with beads and sequins worked in.

I encircled the widest part of the hips with lace. Resist the temptation to glue lace around the waist; the fabric won't stretch anymore and you won't be able to get the dress off the doll.

I took advantage of the scallops in the lace to design the tiara, choker, fan and slippers. The bit of silver rickrack is for looping the fan around the doll's wrist. The slippers require fabric paint and felt to make the soles. You'll also need Velcro for the tiara and choker.

"*My but Gregory has such strange dreams. Perhaps it's not such a great idea to go skiing right now.*"

Spellbound

Materials for December Dream

December Dream Tiara and Choker

The tiara (top) and choker (bottom) are both made from short strips of lace. Put small pieces of Velcro on the ends. The tiara is decorated with a single feather glued behind the lace and a button on the front.

December Dream Fan

Top Left: Cut a small triangle of fabric.
Top Center: Glue a loop of rickrack to the bottom tip. Glue on a feather so that the main rib is on the fabric and the rest floats above the top side.
Top Right: Add more feathers if desired.
Bottom Left and Center: Glue on a bit of lace to hide the ribs of the feathers.
Bottom Right: Flip the fan over and glue lace on the front. Decorate with a button.

December Dream Slippers

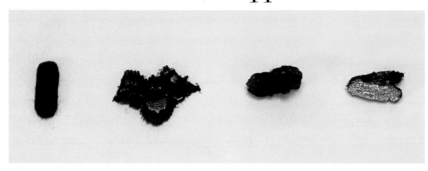

Far Left: Cut an oval of felt that is the size of the doll's foot.
Left Center: Cut a piece of lace using the V part of the scallop.
Right Center: Glue the ends of the lace under the felt sole with the tip of the V at the toe.
Far Right: Glue another oval of felt on the sole. If desired, cover the sole with fabric paint.

Perennial Pink

This dress with a built-in cape takes advantage of the full length of a child's stocking. With a longer stocking, you can make both the dress and cape longer. The doll is wearing Summer-Style booties made with metallic woven fabric instead of knit fabric.

Perennial Pink Dress

1 Cut the leg from a stocking. Place the open end next to the doll where you want the hem to be. Make a horizontal slit about 1" (2.5cm) long for the neck opening, and two ¹/₂" (1.3cm) long slits for the armholes. The armholes should be about ¹/₂" (1.3cm) below the neck opening and about 3" (7.62cm) apart.

2 **Right:** Put the dress on the doll. The long part of the stocking hangs behind it to form a cape. Seal the edges of the armholes with nail polish or fabric paint. For this dress, I coated the entire upper chest with nail polish. Then I glued a string of sequins around the neckline, hem and bottom of the cape.

 Left: To make the belt, hem a narrow strip of fabric that's long enough to tie behind the doll's back. This belt is decorated with a string of sequins.

"Cary should at least have given me a hint. I mean, rock climbing on our honeymoon."

North by Northwest

Off-Season

This is the Perennial Pink dress, only it has a longer dress and shorter cape. To make the high neckline, glue ribbon to the front of the neckline. Let about ½" (1.3cm) of extra ribbon hang free at both sides. Secure the ends of the ribbon behind the doll's neck with Velcro. The belt is a piece of ribbon tied behind the doll's back.

Off Season Hat

To make this stretchy cap, cut the bottom 4" (10.2cm) off the stocking. Tie a knot in the closed end. Roll the open end under to make a hem. You can secure the hem with glue or fabric paint, but it's not necessary. Put the hat on the doll and glue a button or tiny flower next to the knot.

"Basil knows how much I adore dogs. But there's something about dogs and fog that gives me the willies."

Hound of the Baskervilles

Leap Year

The top of this dress is formed by two long strips twisted around each other and pulled around the shoulders. There are many other ways to drape the strips and create different looks. Try them crossed behind the back, looped under and over the shoulders or secured behind the neck with Velcro.

"When Buster mentioned a train ride, I pictured first class on the Orient Express. Next time he asks me out, I'll send a stunt double!"

The General

1 Cut a piece from a stocking leg about 4" (10.2cm) longer than the doll's height. Cut the top 6" (15.2cm) from the back side of the stocking. Slit the front side to make a V shape.

2 Put the stocking on the doll and twist the legs of the V around each other a couple of times.

3 Pull the two legs of the V across the doll's shoulders and around to the back.

4 Glue the legs of the V together behind the doll's back and trim off the excess.

5 Put fabric paint on the raw edges of the dress. You can also highlight some of the folds and twists of the fabric with paint.

Singing Silks

Nothing beats neckties when you're on a budget. Go to a yard sale or thrift shop, drop a couple of clams and walk away with enough fabric for a pure silk evening gown with matching hat, stole, cummerbund, purse and slippers.

I do not recommend swiping neckties from a member of your own household, even if he hasn't worn it for years and you're convinced that all memory of its existence has been swept clean. It's best to ask permission.

Neckties

Like socks, neckties come in the right size and shape for making fashion doll clothes and accessories. Tie designs tilt to the outlandish side of fun, with lavish, intricate patterns scaled just right for miniature outfits. To top it off, neckties possess the same beauty secret as those glamorous Hollywood gowns of yesteryear: the bias cut.

Please note: The following step-by-step instructions for most of the outfits employ two or more different ties.

The three ties on the left are ideal for making fashion doll clothes: They are about 3¹/₂" (8.9cm) wide and made of lightweight fabric. Silk and polyester work equally well. The tie at right is not the best place to start for beginners. It's too wide, so it needs to be cut to size. The heavy fabric won't drape nicely and frays easily. The design and color scheme also present challenges, albeit of a subjective nature.

Of course, ties don't flow down a man's chest like a river of silk. They just kind of hang there. That's because every tie has a piece of stiff interlining that keeps the fabric from stretching. You'll need to remove it before using the tie for doll clothes. In traditional tie construction, the interlining is kept in place by the same loose stitches that hold the back seam together. Snip the threads, unfold the tie and the interlining lifts right out. Remove any tags or loops. Leave the lining (the black fabric) in place.

Bias means that the fabric drapes diagonally, making it stretchy so that it falls in graceful lines without extra tailoring. A bias-cut gown flows sinuously around the female figure like a river of silk. Even when the female figure is only 11¹/₂" (29.2cm) tall, the effect is noticeable.

Glissando

Glissando Gown

1 Remove the interlining from a tie. Fold down the tip at its widest point, place the folded edge level with the top of the doll's head and cut off the excess below her feet. The pipe cleaner and button are for the front bow.

"Eight-inch platform sandals would be just the thing for this outfit, but I'd better stick with flats. Grant is so sensitive about his height these days."

The Incredible Shrinking Man

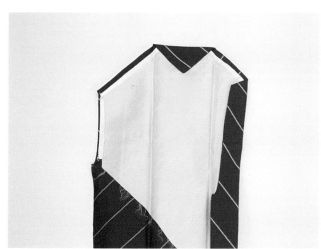

2 Glue down the tip of the tie all along its edges.

3 Glue down just the top ³/₄" (1.9cm) of the sides. The left side, shown here, has been glued. This gives the front bow its sharply defined upper corners.

4 Make two slits for armholes about ³/₄" (1.9cm) long and 3" (7.6cm) apart. The top of the armhole should begin about 2¹/₂" (6.4cm) below the top corner of the tie.

5 Put the dress on the doll and glue the back seam from top to bottom. If your tie is wide, trim the excess fabric.

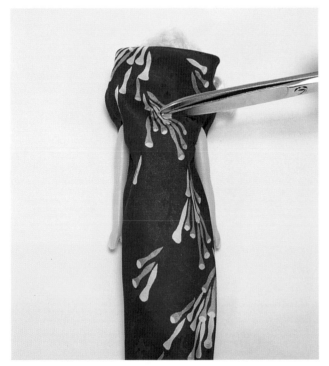

6 To start the front bow, make a little hole in the center of the chest.

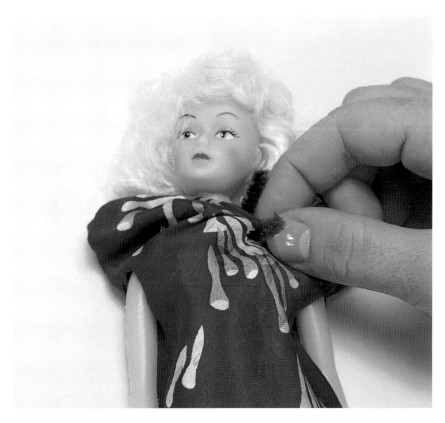

7 Pass a piece of pipe cleaner through the hole. Pinch and pleat the middle of the neckline down and tightly twist the pipe cleaner to hold it.

8 Glue the ends of the bow down to the shoulders. A button is glued in the center to hide the pipe cleaner.

Glissando Hat

1 **Left:** Use the next 4" (10.2cm) long piece of tie after making the dress.

Center: Glue the seam closed and hem both ends.

Right: Pinch and pleat one end down to meet the other. The pinched end is the top of the hat. Slip a pipe cleaner through the hat and twist it tightly to hold the pleats in place.

2 **Right:** Glue the top of the hat shut on either side of the pipe cleaner. This makes the bow look sharper. The finished hat has a button glued over the pipe cleaner.

Left: Glue a pipe cleaner inside the lower hem. This allows you to pinch the hat onto the doll's hair.

Glissando Muff-Purse

Left: Use a 4" (10.2cm) long piece of tie. Glue the seam shut and hem both ends. On each end, make one small pleat. Secure each pleat with just a dot of glue at the top. This gives the muff its curved shape.

Right: Glue the bottom corners of the muff shut, leaving just enough room to insert the doll's hand and arm.

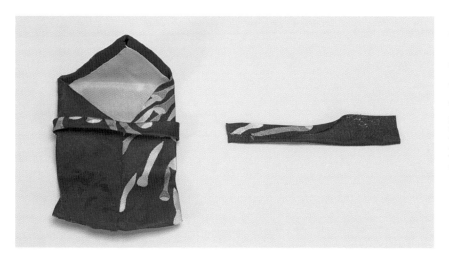

Glissando Clutch

Use the narrowest 3" (7.6cm) of the tie, including the tip. Glue the seam and the end without the tip shut. To make the band around the clutch, hem a piece of tie or use ribbon. Glue just the ends of the band to the back of the clutch. Leave the rest free.

To close the clutch, fold up the lower edge and tuck the tip under the band.

Glissando Slippers

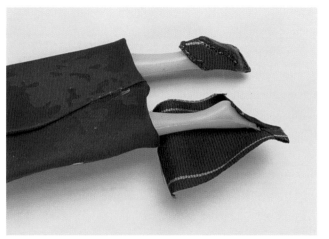

1 These slippers are made from a 1½" × 1¾" (4.5cm × 3.8cm) rectangle of fabric, like the Spring Fling moccasins. The rectangle shown here is cut diagonally from the tie, so it parallels the threads of fabric. I find it easier to handle this way. After you cut the rectangle, turn under one end about ⅛" (.3cm) and glue it down.

2 As with the Spring Fling moccasin, place the rectangle on the bottom of the doll's foot. However, position the hemmed edge just beyond her toe as shown here. Then begin folding down the sides, just as you did for the moccasin. The hemmed edge will overlap itself under the doll's foot. Glue the overlap, then continue folding and gluing up behind the doll's heel, trimming as needed. You'll end up with a bootie. Do not remove it from the doll's foot until completing Step 3.

3 Use fabric paint to trace a line around the doll's ankle. If desired, paint the bottom of the moccasin. When dry, slit through the excess fabric above the line. Remove the bootie and trim away the excess fabric.

Glissando Stole

The remainder of the tie is long enough for a stole. Glue the back seam shut and hem the ends.

Crescendo

This dress is the same as the Glissando except here a cummerbund defines the waist. It's made of an 8" (20.3cm) long piece of tie. Glue the back seam of the piece shut, glue the ends shut and drape it firmly around the doll's waist and upper hips so that it crosses in front. You'll need two little pieces of Velcro to secure the cross.

Crescendo Hat

This is the Glissando hat with a bow made of fabric from the tie.
Left: To make the bow, cut a 2" (5.1cm) long piece of tie. Glue the seam and hem the ends about ½" (1.3cm). Pinch it in the middle and secure it with a twist of wire. Glue a piece of tie or ribbon over the wire.
Center: Pull the two sides of the bow together at the top, and secure them with a dot of glue. The button is optional.

Crescendo Booties

"I thought the job was to deliver bottles of perfume. I was misled. But at least Yves is a good conversationalist."

Wages of Fear

These are the Glissando Slippers. Instead of tracing around the ankle with fabric paint, glue a piece of tie or ribbon around the bootie while it's still on the doll's foot. Then slit through the fabric above, remove the bootie and trim off all of the excess.

Diminuendo

This dress is similar to the Glissando except the back seam is not glued all the way up. It is left open above the hips. Velcro holds it closed at the neckline. This back opening allows you to make the neckline smaller. For this dress, I glued the ends of the bow flat across the shoulders.

The back seam is secured at the top with Velcro.

"Poor Dana. Talk about a bad day at the office. But look on the bright side. At least we ended up on the same rock."

Crack In the World

Diminuendo Stole and Cummerbund

Right: The stole is cut from a 20" (50.8cm) long piece of tie, broader at one end than the other. It has two layers of lace glued all around the edge from behind.

Left: The cummerbund is a piece of tie long enough to fit around the doll's waist with a ½" (1.3cm) overlap. It's held together in back with Velcro.

Adagio

This dress dispenses with the front bow in favor of a flat collar. It starts like the Glissando gown, but instead of pinching the excess fabric into a bow, fold it down straight across under the doll's chin. Glue it in place all along the edge.

Since the neckline opening is very small, make this dress with a Velcro opening in back like the Diminuendo gown.

Attractive in retreat as well as advance.

The fringe has a fluid drape. The beads are from a spray of gilt berries. I left the stems intact so I could wind them around each other, and secure the whole cluster with a minimum of glue.

"If I must be handcuffed to somebody and forced to tramp around the moors at all hours of the night, please let it be with Robert."

The 39 Steps

Adagio Jacket

1 **Left:** Cut one piece of tie long enough to go from the doll's fingertips, up her arm, around her back and down her other arm to her fingertips.

Center: Open up the fabric and hem the ends, gluing thoroughly. The doll's fingers will catch in any loose pockets in the hem.

Right: Fold up the tie again. Glue the back seam only 1" (2.5cm) or so from each end. Leave an opening about 4" (10.2cm) long in the center (as marked by pins).

2 Glue the cuffs partly shut. Leave just enough open to admit the doll's hand.

3 Glue fringe all along the bottom edge of the jacket.

Adagio Hat

1 **Left:** Use the last 4" (10.16cm) of tie, including the tip.

Left Center: Glue a twist-tie or a piece of pipe cleaner inside the bottom edge.

Right Center: Fold up the raw edge and glue it over the twist-tie.

Right: Glue fringe all around the bottom edge.

2 Twist the tip of the tie around the bottom part of the hat.

3 Glue the tip down to the front of the hat. The finished hat has a spray of berries glued on it.

Adagio Bow

The front bow has Velcro behind the top corners, so it can be pulled high under the doll's chin and secured behind her neck.

Pianissimo

You can buy feathers by the bag at most craft shops. They're inexpensive and a little goes a long way. Full-size feathers break the illusion created by the miniature outfits, but you can scale them down by hiding the main rib under a ribbon or string of sequins. It also helps if you clip off the stiff parts at the tip, and just use the fluffy lower part.

Feathers and trimmings

Pianissimo Hat

This is the Adagio hat, but it is made from a 15" (38cm) long piece of tie. Twist the upper part of the hat into a long rope. Dot with glue as you twist to hold it in place. Then glue the rope around the bottom part of the hat. For this hat, I left the top 1" (2.5cm) free to point up, and glued a single feather behind.

"Jean-Paul had done a very bad thing. Maybe he put aluminum cans in with the plastics. Whatever. I turned him in."

Breathless

Pianissimo Gauntlet-Stole

This uses a 12" (30.5cm) long piece of tie. For the gauntlet part, hem one end, glue it shut and fold it over to form a tube just wide enough to admit the doll's arm. Glue it in place along the edge. Hem the other end and glue a row of feathers to the inside. Then glue it shut.

Instead of a front bow, the excess fabric is folded down under the chin and glued in place.

Forte

This is the Adagio gown, but the front fold is angled up instead of straight across. Combined with the oversized, bow-shaped hat, the effect is surreal in keeping with the dreamy pattern of the fabric.

You can find prestrung rhinestones at some fabric shops, or snip them from an old piece of jewelry. Hammer-on rhinestones are another possibility. Gluing them on individually is too messy. The loop of elastic shown here is for the hat. The glitter trim is for the fan.

To make the asymmetrical neckline, fold the excess fabric down on one side of the doll's chest, and hold it in place with a dot of glue.

Forte Fan

"Joseph said he'd show me a side of Vienna I'd never seen before. Oh, yeah? I'll show him a dry cleaning bill he's never seen before."

The Third Man

Left: Cut the last 2" (5.1cm) from the tie, including the tip.
Center: Glue feathers or lace to the inside of the raw edge, then glue it shut. Glue a piece of ribbon around the edge.
Right: Glue the sides together below the ribbon.

Forte Hat

1 **Top Left:** Cut a 6" (15.2cm) long section of tie, hem the ends, glue them shut and pinch the middle together. Hold the pinch in place with a pipe cleaner, and cover it with a hemmed piece of tie or ribbon. Do not glue down the loose ends yet.

　Top Right: Turn the bow over, glue a loop of elastic to the underside and glue down the loose ends over the elastic.

　Bottom: Finished hat with elastic glued in place.

2 Glue some long feathers to one side, then glue some shorter feathers to the other. A string of rhinestones hides the untidy area where the two groups of feathers meet.

Moderato

You find the Perfect Tie. You make the Perfect Gown. Then you discover that, if you were working under the Perfect Light, you would have noticed that huge stain before. But, as any doll worth her salt knows, you can turn the situation around by wearing the dress backwards.

The stand-up collar starts off like a Glissando gown until Step 3. At this step, the upper corners of the Glissando gown are glued together at the uppermost 1/2" (1.3cm). For the Moderato, keep gluing almost all the way down. Leave an opening just large enough to go around the doll's neck. As with the Diminuendo gown, the seam is secured at the top with Velcro.

Moderato Dress

The front seam is open above the hipline. Secure the top with Velcro.

Moderato Hat

Left: Cut a piece of tie about 6" (15.2cm) long. Hem both ends. Starting at one end, make a pleat all the way around. Glue it in place with three or four dots of glue—gluing it all the way around can get too messy. **Right:** Repeat the procedure for as many pleats as will fit, then glue the top end shut. Then glue a piece of pipe cleaner inside the bottom edge.

"I knew William would never have time to walk that dog. Well thank goodness it isn't a Great Dane, or I'll end up flat on my face one of these days."

The Thin Man

Andantino

This dress accommodates ties with patterns that have an obvious one-way design. The boatmen drifting serenely past the houses would look rather uncomfortable upside down, which is how they would have appeared if the tie had been used to make the Glissando dress and its variations.

On half of the kimono jacket, the design does appear upside down. I got away with it here because I used a piece of tie that did not have give-aways like people or houses. Alternatively, you can cut the piece of tie in two equal parts, invert one part and glue it back to the other.

Andantino Dress

1 Cut a piece of tie that reaches from the doll's ankles (at the tie's broadest point) to her shoulders.

"Kevin's been going on about those overgrown vegetables for hours, and he hasn't said a thing about my new dress."

    Invasion of the Body Snatchers

2 In addition to removing the interlining, cut out the lining of the tie to prevent the doll's feet from snagging on it. Trim it about 1/4" (.6cm) away from the stitching. Glue the edges down if they puff out after trimming.

3 **Left:** To hem the bottom edge, glue the tip of the tie to the inside, then glue about the first ³/₄" (1.9cm) of the corners.

Right: Hem the top edge, and glue the back seam from the hipline down. Use Velcro to secure the top of the seam.

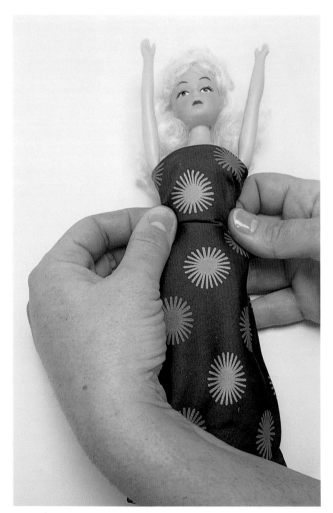

This is how the dress looks before tailoring.

4 To give the dress a fitted waistline, pinch the fabric at the doll's sides...

...and fold the pinch of fabric toward the doll's back. Then glue it in place.

Andantino Hat

Left: Cut a 6" (15.2cm) long piece of tie. Hem one end and glue a piece of pipe cleaner or a twist-tie to the inner edge.

Right: Tightly roll the other end. Hold it in place with a few dots of glue as you roll. Stop rolling when there's still enough hat left to fit over the doll's head.

Andantino Jacket

1 This is an Adagio jacket with hanging sleeves. Use a 15" (38.1cm) long piece of tie. Glue the back seam shut, except for a 4" (10.2cm) long section in the center. Also leave two ³⁄₄" (1.9cm) long sections unglued for the cuff openings. The unglued sections are shown here, marked with pins.

2 Glue the ends of the sleeves shut. Put the jacket on the doll. If the back of the jacket sticks out, make a small pleat in the bottom edge at each side.

Tranquillo

The blue part of this outfit is a sleeveless romper. Like the Andantino dress, the romper uses a tie right side up, so it's good for fabric with an obvious one-way design. The cummerbund, jacket and hat are made from a second tie.

Tranquillo Romper

1 Use a piece of tie that reaches from the doll's knees (at its broadest point) up to her shoulders. Cut out the lining as was done with the Andantino dress.

2 Unfold the tie and lay the doll facedown on it. Her chin should be at the top edge. Pull the tip of the tie through her legs and up over her lower back.

"Now that Sean's given me back my horse, everything is going to be just perfect."

Marnie

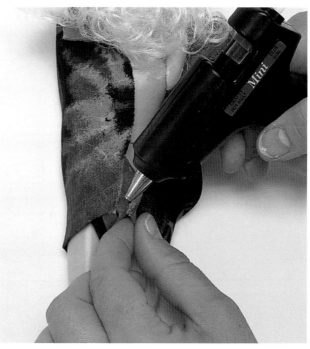

3 Pull the two sides of the tie around to the back…

…Then glue them behind the doll's back. If your tie is wide, the sides may overlap, which is fine.

4 Turn the doll faceup and hem the top edge. It should reach comfortably over the doll's chest and under her arms. Use Velcro to secure the top of the back seam.

This is the finished romper, decorated with a single flower. The complete ensemble has a cummerbund made in a contrasting fabric.

Tranquillo Hat

The showy hat is a good opportunity to use up short scraps of lace. A single flower makes a ready-made rosette.

This hat has no crown.
Top Left: Start with a plastic coffee can lid.
Top Center: Cut the plastic into a donut with the hole big enough to fit loosely around the doll's head. Glue the donut on an open piece of tie. Trim the excess fabric.
Top Right: Repeat this step to cover both sides of the plastic.
Bottom Left: Glue your best lace to the outer and inner edges of the donut. This is the top side of the hat.
Bottom Right: Turn the hat over and glue narrow lace or plain ribbon around the edges.

Tranquillo Jacket

1 This is the Adagio jacket, made with a 24" (61cm) long piece of tie. When you put the jacket on the doll, scrunch up the sleeves to get her hands through the cuffs. This creates the illusion of ruffled sleeves.

2 Put the jacket on the doll and let the sleeves hang loosely. Glue lace in an oval bordered by the doll's neck and shoulders, and by the bottom edge of the jacket. The lace used here is 1" (2.5cm) wide.

4 Hanky Panky

Peasant chic was big in the 1970s. So was granny style. It's only a matter of time before fashion fossils become tomorrow's hot looks. Your doll can get a jump on the rest of the pack if you can spare a few odds and ends from your linen closet such as napkins, dish cloths, scarves, doilies and even sleeves from an old shirt.

Ohio

The easiest place to start is a woven plaid napkin, preferably with a fringe or some other decoration around the edges. Woven plaid fabric looks good on both sides, so it can fold over to make a shawl collar and other embellishments.

The peach napkin is 16¾" (42.5cm) square with a ¾" (1.9cm) fringe. You can use napkins several inches bigger or smaller, and they can be rectangles instead of squares.

Woven plaid napkins are a good place to start. So are woven dish towels as long as the "wrong" side looks attractive.

Ohio Dress

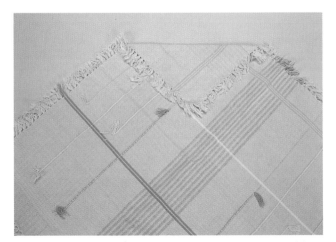

1 Lay the napkin flat, right side up if there is one. Fold down one corner to form a triangle. The triangle should measure about 3" (7.6cm) from the fold to the bottom tip. This makes the collar.

"A date with Rod…to go bird watching. How romantic."

THE BIRDS

2 Make two ³/₄" (1.9cm) long slits for armholes. They should be at or just below the fold line and about 2" (5.1cm) apart.

3 Put the dress on the doll with the opening in front. The collar drapes down in back like a shawl. Following the drape of the collar, fold over the front sides. Adjust the neckline so the two sides overlap about ¹/₂" (1.3cm). Secure the top edge with Velcro.

4 Glue the remainder of the front opening, from the hips down to the bottom edge.

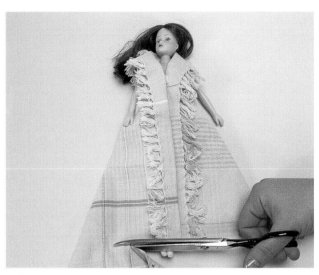

5 To give the dress a gently curved hem, lay it flat and trim across the bottom.

6 Then turn the doll on her side, lay the dress flat again and trim off the corners.

7 If the neckline won't fall flat, glue down a little pleat on each side near the front seam.

8 Cut the fringe off a leftover piece of napkin. Hem and glue it on the dress along the bottom edge...

9 ...and around the collar. In the finished dress, the fringe has been trimmed short around the collar, apron and front seam, so that it doesn't overwhelm the outfit.

Ohio Shawl and Apron

Top: The shawl is a corner of the napkin, hemmed along the bottom.
Bottom: The apron is a smaller corner of napkin. To make the waistband, cut a piece of fringe from some leftover napkin. Glue it to the bottom of the triangle and put Velcro on the ends.

Ohio Hat

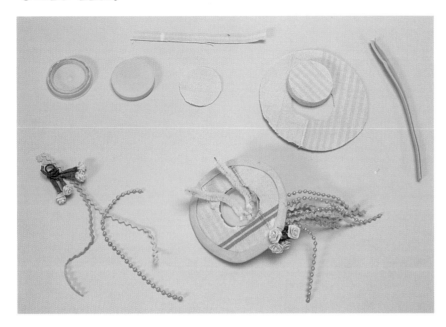

Top Left: The crown of the hat is a plastic cap from a milk jug. Trim the cap, if necessary, so its top is flush with its side.

Top Center: Glue a strip of napkin around the side of the milk cap, and a circle on top.

Top Right: The brim is a donut-shaped piece of plastic covered with napkin, just like the Tranquillo hat from chapter three. Glue the milk cap over the hole. Then glue a piece of lace or ribbon around the brim.

Bottom Left: To start the decoration, glue on a few strands of prestrung pearls or baby rickrack. Then glue on some miniature flowers. Some are clipped off their stems to cut down on excess greenery.

Bottom Right: Glue a pipe cleaner inside the hat.

The finished hat. A string of pearls hides the seam between crown and brim.

Robinson Run

If your napkin is striped, the stripes will make a T intersection at the front seam. To avoid this cut off the entire collar. Glue ribbon or lace around the neckline and put the dress on backwards. The stripes make an attractive diagonal sweep across the front, while the offending T intersection is hidden behind.

Since the collar is cut off and the seam is behind the doll, this outfit does not need to be made with a fringed napkin. Any square of fabric will do.

The T intersection at the back seam.

Robinson Run Accessories

Pom-poms are a good accent for the puffy ribbon. They are readily available at craft shops in a wide range of sizes and colors.

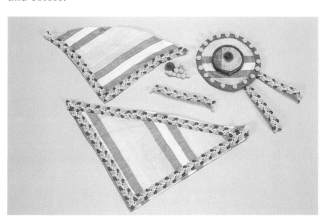

"Claude, what do you think of my new outfit? Claude? Now where did he go? He always seems to disappear just when I need him!"

THE INVISIBLE MAN

Beaver Run

This dress is made from a dish towel. While the fabric is not reversible, the "wrong" side is still attractive. It appears on the collar and alongside the front seam, and provides an interesting counterpoint to the right side.

Shawls and aprons made from bulky dish towels seem to weigh down the outfit, so I skipped them in favor of the fur muff.

I used fur as a trimming on Beaver Run because it has enough presence to stand out against the heavily textured towel. The milk cap and elastic are for the hat.

"I'd follow Errol through anything: rain, snow, sleet, more snow. If he always gets his man, then by gum, I'll get mine."

NORTHERN PURSUIT

Beaver Run Hat

Upper Right: Start with the plastic cap from a milk jug. Glue a loop of elastic or pipe cleaner inside.
Lower Right: Cut a long strip of fringe from the dish towel. Pleat it around the milk cap, gluing as you go.
Upper Left: The finished hat has fur glued around the edge. The fur puff in the middle is a strip of fur glued in half lengthwise (wrong sides together), and then folded in half again.

Beaver Run Muff

The muff is a tube of fur fabric. If you buy the fur in strips, you may need to glue two strips together to make one wider piece.

Allegheny

I don't know about you, but I find it difficult, if not impossible, to cut up antique linens. Then again, it seems a shame to let beautiful old hankies molder away in a box. Loungewear is one solution. This dress preserves the entire crocheted hem of the handkerchief by letting the excess form a train behind.

I folded down the front edges of the hanky close to the crochet work, then glued them together edge to edge with no overlap. This allows the crochet work to form an uninterrupted panel across the front. I disguised the front seam with prestrung pearls.

Because the front seam has no overlap, there is no opportunity to use Velcro. Just glue the entire seam. Leave the neck opening wide enough to slip the dress off the doll's shoulders. For the sake of modesty, you can provide her with a lace camisole like those described in chapter five.

Hankies like these are good for loungewear.

"Now I don't mind being an underpaid waitress at a ramshackle hotel in the middle of the desert during a war when the only guests are enemy officers. Franchot is here!"

FIVE GRAVES TO CAIRO

The beads on the front seam are prestrung, so you don't have to glue the entire length—just a few dots will do. The camisole is a piece of lace secured behind the doll's back with Velcro.

To give the dress a tighter waist, pinch it on either side. Pull this excess fabric to the back and glue it in place.

Monongahela

For the front seam of this dress, overlap the two sides without folding them down first. The effect is like a wrap dress.

After the corner of the scarf is faced as shown at the bottom of page 79, the rest of the dress is similar to the Ohio dress. Make two slits for armholes, put the dress on the doll and turn down the collar in back. Then, instead of folding down the two sides of the front seam, just lap one over the other. Secure the seam at the top with Velcro, and glue the rest of the seam from the hips down to the toes. Leave the hem of the scarf intact to get the royal train effect.

The waistline is tailored like the Allegheny dress. Pinch the excess fabric at the sides of the waistline, fold them back and glue them behind the doll's back.

The mood of the dress is directly related to the design of the scarf. Paisleys and flowers are good for classic gowns.

"Well I didn't want to walk into that crummy little cafe either, but Paul insisted."

CASABLANCA

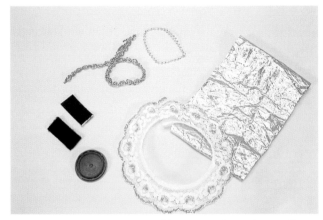

Many scarves are not reversible, so you'll need a small piece of fabric, like the metallic gold pictured here, to make a facing for the collar. The hat uses a milk cap, lace and small scrap of fabric. The Velcro is for securing the front seam of the dress.

Like the Allegheny dress, undergarments may be required. Pictured at left is a short slip with a puff of lace at the back to fluff out the skirt of the dress. At right is a strapless camisole.

Monongahela Hat

1 **Left:** Use the cap of a milk jug with the edges trimmed off if necessary.
   Right: Cut two slits in the cap, and pass a ½" (1.3cm) wide ribbon or hemmed strip of fabric through from the bottom.

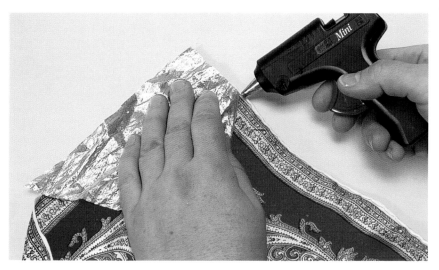

2 **Left:** Cover the cap with fabric.
   Right: Hem a piece of gathered lace on both ends, and glue it all around the side of the cap. This picture shows the rear of the hat. The two hemmed ends of lace do not connect. This allows the lace to accommodate the curve of the doll's head.

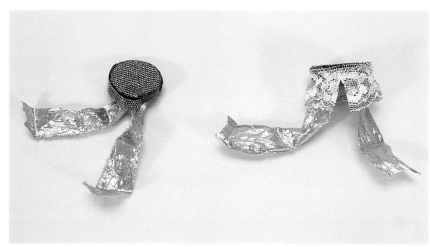

For the collar, glue a triangle of fabric to the wrong side of the scarf, all along the two hemmed edges. The triangle should extend about 8" (20.3cm) down these edges. Leave the bottom of the triangle free.

Loyalhanna

This design is good for scarves with a lot of detail concentrated along the hem and little or no detail in the center. You can use either a reversible or nonreversible scarf. The right side of the fabric will show up on the bodice, and the wrong side will show up on the skirt.

Embroidered hankies are also suitable for this dress.

"Bela's been so moody. Maybe it's because he's afraid of going to the dentist."

DRACULA

Loyalhanna Dress

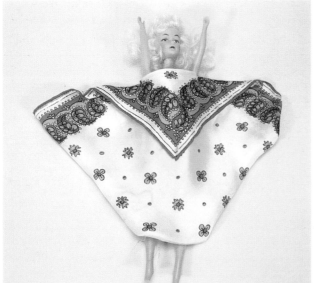

1 Lay the scarf on the doll, right side down. Fold down one corner until the tip reaches her hips.

2 Turn the doll facedown, and bring the sides of the scarf to her back. Trim off the excess fabric, leaving enough to overlap a seam down the center back.

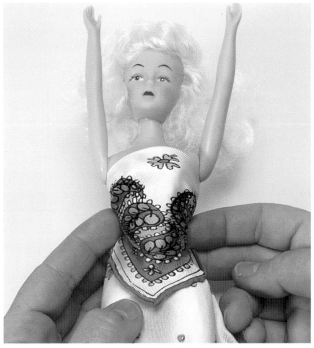

3 Glue the back seam from the hips down. Secure the top of the seam with Velcro.

4 Tailor the waistline by taking a pinch of fabric from each side and gluing it behind the doll's back. Try to pick up just the top layer of fabric, leaving the bottom layer to fall free.

Loyalhanna Hat

Cut a 1" (2.5cm) wide strip of fabric from the hem of an extra piece of scarf. Glue one end to a loop of elastic. Start pleating the fabric and glue each pleat to the loop until the fabric makes a complete circle. The sequins hide the untidy area in the center of the hat.

Kiskiminetas

The blouse and skirt are each made from a 9"
(22.9cm) diameter doily. Compared to the other
materials in this book, new doilies of this size can
be a little pricey—about two or three dollars each.
When experimenting with doily fashions, you can
spare the expense of making a mistake by tracing
the doily on a scrap of fabric and using the scrap
for practice.

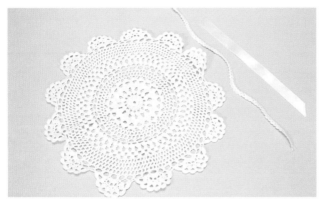

New doilies are available at craft and fabric shops as well
as household linens shops. The prestrung sequins are for
trimming the neckline, and the wide ribbon is for the
waistband.

*"A long
vacation with
James. How sweet.
If only he had
alerted me to the
fact that it would
all be underground.
I would have worn brown."*

A JOURNEY TO THE CENTER OF THE EARTH

Kiskiminetas Blouse

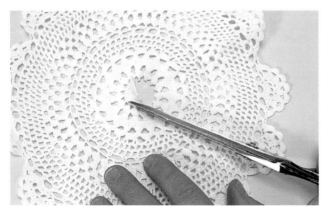

1 Remove enough of the center to allow the doily to slip
over the doll's head. Only remove a little because the
threads stretch a lot.

2 Put the doily over the doll's head, adjust the neckline
and secure it by gluing a string of sequins around it.
Keep the neckline in position as you glue, so that it stays
wide enough to fit over the doll's head.

3 To make the sleeves, drape the doily over the doll's arms. Pinch it together around the doll's wrist, and hold it in place with a dot of glue. It's possible to glue the sleeve together all the way up the arm, but I don't recommend it. I did it once and the doll kept snagging her thumb in the crochet work.

4 For the waistband, glue a piece of ribbon to the front of the doily over the doll's waistline. Leave the ends of the ribbon loose. Pass each loose end through to the underside of the doily and behind the doll's back.

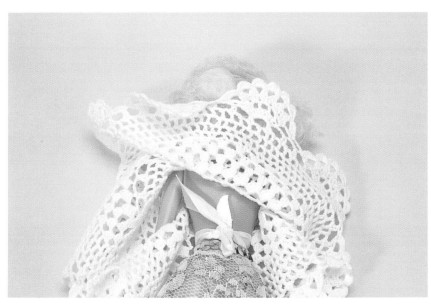

5 Tie the loose ends of the waistband behind the doll's back. Velcro can be used as a substitute if desired.

Kiskiminetas Skirt

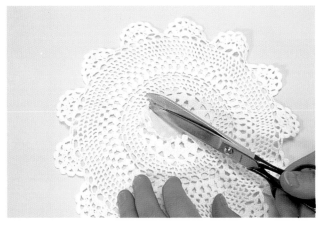 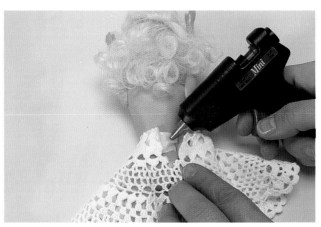

1 Remove the center of the doily. Then cut a 2" (5.1cm) long slit starting from the center. Dot the edges of the slit with glue to keep them from unraveling.

2 Drape a piece of ribbon around the doll's waist and secure it behind with Velcro. Put the doily on the doll, and glue the inner edge of the doily around the ribbon.

Kiskiminetas Hat

This hat calls for a juice bottle cap, some fabric or pieces of lace to cover it and a decoration like the clip-on earring pictured here.

Upper Left: Glue fabric or lace all around the side of the bottle cap, pleating it over the top. As shown here, I glued a layer of fabric on first so the green cap wouldn't show through the white lace.

Upper Right: Glue an extra piece of fabric or lace in the middle of the cap. This will hide the untidy area in the center.

Lower Right: These two scraps of lace were salvaged from the doily and strip of lace used to make the hat. Either one is fine for gluing on the center of the hat.

Shenango

This outfit is a doily blouse made from a 10" (25.4cm) diameter doily. It's long enough to be worn as a minidress. The boots are made from a scrap of lace, using the same method as the Summer-Style bootie from chapter two.

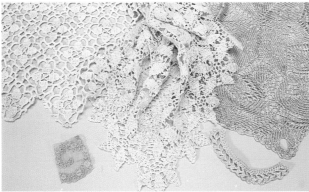

Top: Old doilies of practically any size and shape will do for the veiled hat.
Lower Left: An extra scrap of lace for the boots.
Lower Right: A piece of narrow lace for the neckline, waistband and choker necklace.

"I guess I'll come along on Gregory's boring old fishing trip."
MOBY DICK

Shenango Hat

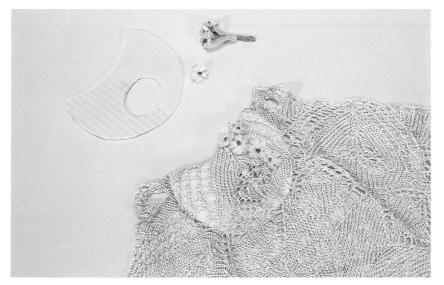

Upper Left: Make a hat brim from a piece of plastic and cover it with fabric. The brim can be any shape. The hole should be big enough to fit over the doll's head.
Lower Right: Glue the doily over the brim. Do not stretch it. When you put the hat on the doll, the top of her head will stretch the doily to form the crown of the hat.
Top Right: This hat was decorated with miniature flowers snipped off their stems.

Neshannock

One day while I was sorting through a box of linens, I came upon a beautiful silk shirt. I don't know why it was in with my linens, but that's the reason gowns made from shirtsleeves are included in this chapter.

You'll need a shirtsleeve with a cuff. The cuff can be plain, frilled, lacy, wide or narrow. The sleeve should be about equal to the doll's height, including the cuff.

Left: This dress uses a sleeve with a plain cuff, about 2¹/₂" (6.4cm) wide. When buttoned, it's about 4¹/₂" (11.4cm) long (10" [25.4cm] long from end to end when unbuttoned).

Right: Save the button side of the front placket for the stole and cummerbund. You'll also need the collar (not pictured here) for the hat. The buttons and feathers are to decorate the stole and hat.

"Why, there's Kirk, hanging out in the fields again. What if I go ahead and sneak up behind…he'll never hear me, what with all those crows making such a racket."

Lust For Life

Neshannock Dress

1 Button the cuff, lay it flat with the button in the center and slit two armholes in either side. The armholes should be about ³/₄" (1.9cm) long. The top of the armhole should be about 1" (2.5cm) from the top of the cuff. Put it on the doll with the button toward the front.

2 Fold the top corners of the cuff over the doll's shoulders, and glue them down in front.

Neshannock Cummerbund

Right: Cut the button side of the front placket off the shirt, leaving an extra ¼" (.6cm) of fabric along the edge. Turn the extra fabric under to make a hem as shown.
Top Left: Put Velcro on the ends.

Neshannock Stole

Top: Hem a 15" (38.1cm) long piece of the front placket, as you did for the cummerbund. Then glue feathers to the wrong side.
Bottom: Glue a ribbon down the center of the wrong side to hide the center rib of the feathers.

Neshannock Hat

Bottom: Cut off a corner of the shirt collar. The bottom edge of the corner should be big enough to fit over the doll's head. Glue a twist-tie or pipe cleaner inside the bottom edge and hem it.
Top: The front of the hat is decorated with feathers and a button.

Laurel

What a gorgeous blouse this was, up until that piece of barbecued chicken fell on it. I was devastated, but at least it could still be enjoyed by someone less accident prone than I.

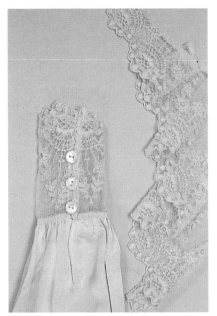

Left: The lace cuff is about 3½" (8.9cm) wide, and 3½" (8.9cm) long when buttoned (7" [17.8cm] long unbuttoned).
Right: The shirt had a lace collar big enough for an overskirt and a generously veiled hat.

"Last night I dreamed...that Laurence sold that big old jalopy of a house and bought me a spiffy minimalist condo on the French Riviera for a wedding present!"
REBECCA

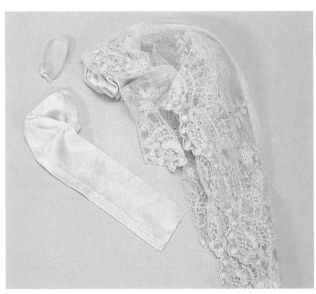

Laurel Hat

Left: This is similar to the Loyalhanna hat. It's a long strip of fabric pleated and glued onto a loop of elastic. I used a 1½" (3.8cm) wide strip of fabric from the bottom edge of the blouse to take advantage of its neatly executed machine-stitched hem. To give the hat an asymmetrical shape, I bunched a few pleats close together on one side and glued them down to the edge.
Right: The finished hat has a long piece of lace from the shirt collar glued on top.

Laurel Dress

1 This dress is the Neshannock dress, except with a pinched-in waist instead of a cummerbund. Start by slitting two armholes in the cuff, and put it on the doll.

2 Fold the corners of the cuff over the shoulders and glue in place.

3 To tailor the waistline, draw a pinch of fabric from each side at the waist, and glue it to the back.

Laurel Overskirt

This is made from a piece of the lace collar, glued in a cone shape, with the top 2" (5.1cm) of the back seam open. A ribbon is glued around the top edge.

Somerset

Shirtsleeves with a frilled cuff like this one open up new design possibilities. This cuff is 1¹/₂" (3.8cm) wide.

Somerset Dress

Do not cut armholes in the cuff. Put the sleeve on the doll. The cuff will go under her arms and over her chest. Pull it up over her shoulders and glue the two edges of the cuff together, front to back. For short sleeves, glue this seam from the base of the doll's neck to her shoulder. For longer sleeves, continue gluing down the arm as far as the fabric will reach.

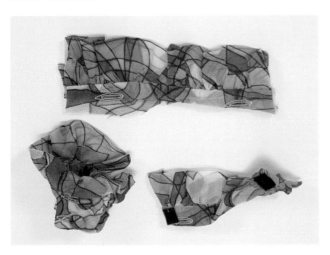

"It's bad enough I dressed for a Sunday picnic and haven't even seen the sun all day, but Burt and Clark won't stop bickering and they're spoiling all my fun!"

RUN SILENT, RUN DEEP

Somerset Hat and Cummerbund

Top: The ruffle from the other cuff is long enough for a cummerbund or hat. This shirt had a ruffled collar, so there was enough for both.

Bottom Left: For the hat, glue the cuff in a cone shape with the ruffle at the bottom. Then glue the top of the cone shut.

Bottom Right: The cummerbund is made from a piece of the ruffled collar. The unruffled edge has been hemmed.

Redstone

I try to avoid obvious giveaways as to scale, such as the standard blue rickrack pictured here, but in this case, the bold plaid fabric is strong enough to balance it out.

Clarion

This dress is made from an embroidered hanky. It is hemmed with extra lace cut from the hanky. The shoulder straps are two short pieces of lace from the hanky, hemmed and glued in place. The hat is decorated with a button glued on top of a few petals.

"I told Jimmy it's not nice to snoop."

REAR WINDOW

"If only Orson would kick out for one of those neat 3-D puzzles, things would be different between us."

CITIZEN KANE

5

Anything Goes

Walk into any craft supply shop and you'll find lace, felt, ribbon, flowers, feathers, beads, polymer clay and other offbeat materials that aren't usually associated with doll clothes. If you favor the unusual for your dolls, craft shops are veritable laboratories for your fashion experiments.

Saraband

Lace alone provides enough material to make anything from lighter-than-air lingerie to elaborate
gowns. Gathered lace is the easiest place to start.
It's already pinched into a shape that follows the
curve of the doll's chest and hips, so it's perfect for
skirts and camisoles.

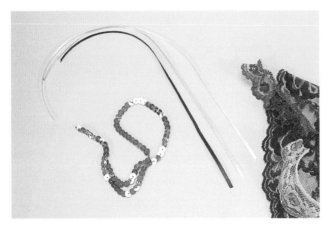

Lace and trimmings

Saraband Skirt

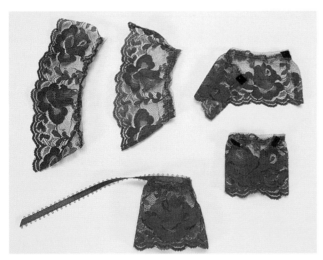

Top Left: Cut a piece of 2" (5.1cm) wide (or wider)
gathered lace, long enough to go around the doll's waist
with about 1" (2.5cm) to spare.
Top Center: Hem both ends of the lace.
Top Right: Put Velcro at the top corner of each end.
Bottom Right: Glue the bottom corners of the skirt
together.
Bottom Left: Glue a piece of ribbon over the waistband.

*"I should have known Howard
wouldn't listen. After all, he never
pays attention to the way I dress.
All right, I'll say it one more time:
Saltwater is not good for plants."*

THE DAY OF THE TRIFFIDS

Saraband Camisole

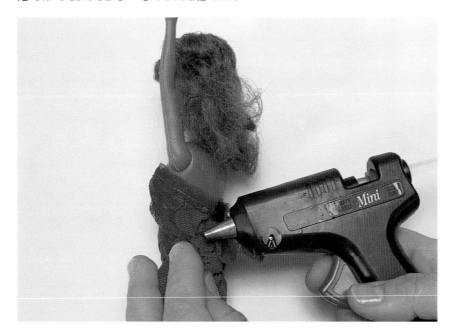

1 Start as if making the Saraband skirt, but this time fit the lace over the doll's chest. Pinch the excess fabric at the sides and glue it down behind the doll's back.

2 **Left:** After tailoring, the back of the camisole may look untidy...
Right: ...so trim off some of the excess fabric or tuck it under.

More With Lace

Wider lace means more excess fabric to glue behind the camisole. Instead of trimming it off, glue a button or flower over it, along with some narrow ribbon or prestrung pearls, and turn it into a bowlike decoration.

"What was I thinking of when I fell for John?"

*DESERT FURY*

"I really shouldn't get on Leslie for the little things. Like the way he dresses."

THE SCARLET PIMPERNEL

Top: The scalloped edge of this lace is overscaled. Let it define the contours of the outfit.

Center: This lace is more in proportion with the doll, but make sure the scallops conform to the lines of the outfit.

Bottom: These tiny scallops would not affect the silhouette of the outfit.

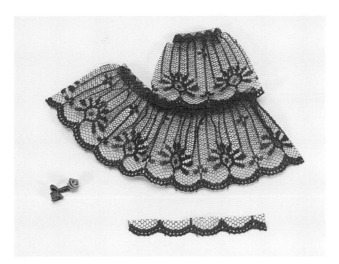

Top: This tiered skirt is just like the Saraband skirt with an extra layer of lace glued all around.

Center and Bottom: The camisole is decorated with a miniature flower snipped from its stem. The scalloped edge of some spare lace was glued to the top hem of the camisole.

"If I was riding on the subway, and all of a sudden somebody hijacked it, I would want to know that somewhere, somehow, Walter was looking after me."

THE TAKING OF PELHAM
ONE TWO THREE

Bolero

Bolero Negligee

Bottom: The negligee is two pieces of equal-length lace glued together along the gathered edges (different lengths are pictured here for clarity). Put Velcro on the waistline at the back, then glue the bottom corner of the skirt. To keep the camisole from puffing out too much, trim or tuck it under. Then secure it at the top with Velcro.
Center: Trim for the waistband.
Top: The bed jacket.

"Chasing an oversized lump of Silly Putty around town is not exactly my idea of a first date, but Steve can make anything feel special."

THE BLOB

Bolero Bed Jacket

Cut a piece of lace long enough to go around the doll's shoulders and behind her back. Glue the ends together to form a loop. Then glue the top of the loop (behind the doll's neck) down to the bottom (behind the doll's back). Just glue the bottom edge of the lace, and leave the gathered edge free. This maneuver forms two short sleeves. Glue ribbon all around the gathered edge.

Cakewalk

Eyelet lace is fabric with holes punched in it. If the holes or "eyes" are not too many or too big, you can use it to make outdoor clothes using the same methods as the lingerie styles. Eyelet lace is not as common as regular lace, but many craft shops carry both flat and gathered eyelet lace.

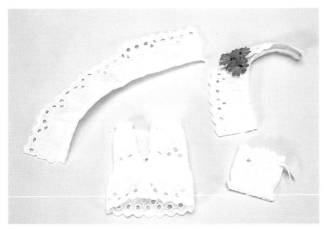

Top Left: Lace with "eyes" concentrated at the bottom edge.

Top Right: The hat is a piece of lace secured behind the head with Velcro. Put it on the doll with the gathered edge down. Fold over one side and glue it in place. Decorate with flowers.

Bottom Right: For the purse, glue a 2" (5.1cm) long piece of lace in a loop. Glue the gathered edge shut. Pass a narrow ribbon through the eyelets to form a drawstring. A string of sequins decorates the bottom.

Bottom Left: This lace is not wide enough for one tier to reach past the doll's hips, so the back seam of the skirt is not glued shut until the second tier.

"A boat ride with Humphrey. How dreamy. But what to wear? Oh, I'll just throw something on. After all, it's not like we'll be gone all day."

THE AFRICAN QUEEN

Maxixe

This outfit layers a white eyelet lace skirt under the sheer purple skirt. The top is halter style.

Maxixe Hat

Left: Gathered lace of any width may be used. This is 1" (2.5cm) wide.

Center: For the crown, glue a short piece of lace in a loop. Then glue the gathered edge shut.

Right: For the brim, glue another piece of lace all around the edge of the crown. If your lace has full gathers, the brim will flare out nicely. If your lace is gathered loosely, you may need to make a few extra pleats in it as you glue it onto the crown.

Bottom: Glue a piece of ribbon around the bottom of the crown.

"I do wish William had let me get to the other side before he knocked that bridge over."

THE BRIDGE ON THE RIVER KWAI

Maxixe Halter Top

1 Start as if you were making the Bolero bed jacket by looping a piece of lace around the doll's shoulders and behind her neck. Instead of gluing the ends together behind her back, secure them with Velcro.

2 Lay a piece of lace across the doll's chest. Glue it to the sides of the halter. Tuck or pinch the lace so it fits snugly over the chest. I put this lace on with the gathered edge up. It also works with the gathered edge down.

3 **Right:** Trim the gathered edges with ribbon.
Left: Pinch and glue the ribbon into a V shape to define the bustline.

Fandango

This is what happens to the Maxixe outfit when you have a lot of extra lace and a bit of extra time on your hands.

The skirt has about ten tiers. To prevent it from flaring out too much, alternate gathered lace with flat lace or ribbon. Once I finished with the tiers, I went back and glued strings of sequins on top.

The top is the Maxixe halter with extra tiers added to the chest. After gluing the first piece of lace across the chest, the extra tiers follow the curve of the shoulder straps. They go under the doll's arms and around to her back.

The hat crown starts with a loop of lace like the Maxixe, only it's big enough to fit over more of the doll's head. Instead of gluing the gathered edge shut, cover the opening with a scrap of lace. The brim uses two tiers of lace instead of just one. Strings of sequins are glued around the underside of the brim.

For the stole, use two 20" (50.8cm) long pieces of lace. Glue the gathered edges together. Cover the seam with a string of sequins.

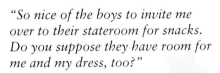

"So nice of the boys to invite me over to their stateroom for snacks. Do you suppose they have room for me and my dress, too?"

A NIGHT AT THE OPERA

Put extra scraps of lace to use.

Hop

Hop Dress

1 Make a Saraband skirt and put it on the doll. Glue one end of a piece of lace to one side of the skirt front. Then cross the lace over the opposite shoulder, and glue it to the back of the skirt.

2 Repeat Step 1 starting with the other side of the skirt.

"Such a storm brewing, and Colin up late again working. He said I shouldn't interrupt, but I'm sure he wouldn't mind me stopping by to show off my new outfit. And I'm just dying to meet his new friend."

FRANKENSTEIN

Top: A hairband trimmed with ribbon, constructed like the Cakewalk hairband.
Bottom: The finished dress (rear view) trimmed with ribbon.

Reel

This is a slight variation on the Hop dress. It takes advantage of the wide ribbon-and-lace border.

Bottom Left: The second tier of lace on the skirt is glued over the first tier, right up to the border.

Right: Instead of gluing the shoulder straps down to the skirt back, guide them around to meet behind the doll's neck and secure them with Velcro. This makes an off-the-shoulder neckline. You may need an extra little piece of lace (top left) to fill in across the doll's chest.

"Speaking of storms, there's something brewing out there. But I'm not afraid as long as Jon is by my side and my best dress is on me."

THE HURRICANE

Minuet

Felt is a marvelous fabric. It doesn't fray and never needs to be hemmed. It's a standard item at craft and fabric stores. The economics work out perfectly, since it comes in small, doll-sized squares, about 12" (30.5cm) or so, which cost just a few cents. One felt square is enough for a complete outfit.

The moccasins are the same as the Spring Fling moccasins from chapter two, with a miniature chili pepper glued on. Felt is rather bulky, so you may need to clip out some of the excess fabric instead of just folding it under.

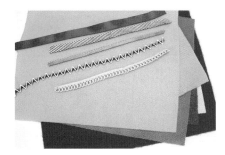

Felt comes in doll-sized pieces like the ones shown here. A few scraps of ribbon and some Velcro are all that's needed to make a dress, hat, and moccasins or booties.

"I know Jimmy will have his hands full transporting a desperate criminal across rugged territory but I won't get in the way. And if we run out of food, we can eat my clothes."

THE NAKED SPUR

Minuet Skirt

1 **Left:** To start the waistband, cut a piece of ribbon long enough to go around the doll's waist, with about 1¹/₂" (3.8cm) to spare.
Center: Hem each end of the ribbon about ¹/₂" (1.3cm).
Right: Put Velcro on the ends.

2 Cut a circle of felt approximately 6" (15.2cm) in diameter. Make a slit from the center to the edge. Then make five or six ¹/₂" (1.3cm) long slits in the center.

3 **Left:** Put the felt skirt on the doll over the waistband. **Right:** Starting in the back, glue the skirt to the waistband.

4 The bodice is made like the top of the Hop dress. Glue two ribbons to the skirt front, cross them in front, draw them over the shoulders and glue them down to the skirt back.

5 Fill in the chest, where needed, with scraps of felt. Then glue a piece of ribbon over the waistband. The fruit decorations are from a set of refrigerator magnets.

After attaching the skirt to the waistband, glue the back seam below the hipline. The seam will overlap quite a bit toward the bottom edge of the skirt. I usually let it overlap and trim off the excess, which makes the skirt fall more gracefully. Otherwise, it stands up in a semicircle. You can also give the skirt a smoother drape by pulling it down firmly and making it stretch over the doll's hips.

Minuet Hat

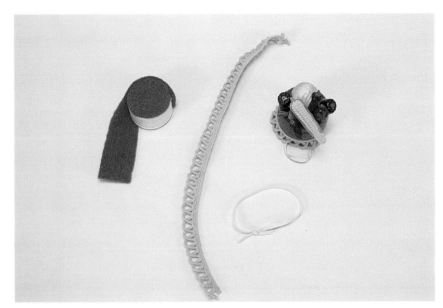

Left: Cover a soda bottle cap with felt.
Center: Glue lace around the bottom edge.
Bottom Right: Make a loop of elastic to fit around the doll's head.
Top Right: Glue the elastic loop inside the hat. Decorate with fruit.

A single flower makes a quick cover-up...

...as does a couple of feathers.

Jig

Dollhouse stores are a great source for unusual decorations. The miniatures can be rather expensive, but you can get good value if you buy items with a lot of little parts, like sets of silverware or the deck of cards shown here.

Bottom Left: After attaching the skirt to the waistband, glue lace or ribbon over it and then decorate it with cards. Lace is also applied to the inside of the bottom edge.
Top Left: The halter top is made like the Maxixe top. A scrap of felt is needed to fill in the chest.
Bottom Right: The halter top with cards glued on.
Top Right: For the hat, tiers of cards are glued on a hairband made from a piece of ribbon (center right) and secured in the back with Velcro.

"If Charlton is going to do that old part-the-waters gag again, then I'll show off my card tricks. Two can play at that game!"

THE TEN COMMANDMENTS

Ragtime

Children's toys are another good source for miniatures. This dress is decorated with parts from a jewelry-making kit. I used a pair of pliers to snip the loops off the charms.

The skirt gets its bell silhouette from slits that go from the hem to the hips. Two are in front and two are in back. The edges of the slits are overlapped and glued, and the excess fabric is trimmed off. Then the seam is covered with rickrack.

Ragtime Hat

Top Left: For the crown, cut a 1½" (3.8cm) wide strip of felt long enough to go around the doll's head, and glue it in a tube.

Bottom Left: For the brim, cut a 4" (10.2cm) diameter circle. Make five or six ½" (1.3cm) slits in the center.

Left Center: Put the crown on the brim. Push the center of the brim up inside the crown. The slits stretch into little triangles. Glue them to the inside of the crown.

Right Center: To shape the crown, cut the top off at an angle. The front of the crown should only be about ½" (1.3cm) tall. Then glue a teardrop-shaped scrap of felt on top.

Top Right: The finished hat.

Bottom Right: To make a rosette, start with a long piece of narrow ribbon. Make little loops in the ribbon, each angled slightly away from the one before, and glue them to the center as you go. Stop when you've make a complete circle of loops.

"Imagine Ray giving up a weekend in the country just to take me shopping on Third Avenue."

THE LOST WEEKEND

Tango

Crummy old jewelry gets one of life's rare second chances when glued on a dress. This outfit uses a variety of pieces: a wide chain-link necklace around the skirt and shoulders, pieces of chain link around the hem and hat, and clip-on earrings (with the clips removed) for the chest and hat.

I used one of those intense nail polish-eating glues to put this outfit together, but you can probably get away with using a glue gun or milder craft glue, especially if the jewelry does not weigh very much.

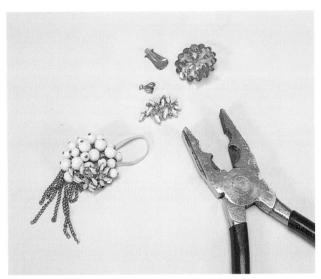

Right: You'll need a pair of heavy pliers to snip the jewelry into pieces.
Lower Left: The hat starts with a single, large clip-on earring with the clip removed. A few extra beads and chain links are added.

"If Marlon thinks I can be impressed by a heap of metal, he can guess again."

THE WILD ONE

Mazurka

Stringing beads involves a needle and thread, so I won't discuss it in these pages. But I can recommend prestrung pearls, which are available at many craft shops. Each pearl is stuck on the thread, so you can cut the strand to any length you please and nothing will fall off. It's difficult to glue the strands down flat, because the glue will show, so I generally use them in places where only their ends need to be glued.

Left: The top is a Saraband camisole made of ½" (1.3cm) wide lace. Strands of pearls are looped under the center front. The pearls along the upper edge are glued only at the back and center. For the center ornament, tear some soft pieces of feather off the main rib and glue a button on top.

Center: The headpiece starts with a hairband made of a ribbon secured in the back with Velcro. Short strands of pearls are glued along the bottom edge in the center, and long strands at the sides. The ends are hidden under a layer of lace.

Right: Prestrung pearls in a wide variety of colors are available at many craft shops. Glittery gathered lace is a good complement for the pearls.

"Robert, a raft, white water and me. Thank the stars for wash-'n-wear."
RIVER OF NO RETURN

Foxtrot

Prestrung pearls are good for making capes and stoles. This a basic sock dress from chapter two except that it's made from the sleeve of a sweater. It sports an attached cape made from prestrung pearls.

The hat is a soda bottle cap covered with fabric. Loops of pearls are glued in front to make a veil. The short strands of pearls in the back are stiff enough to stand up on their own. A loop of pearls glued behind the hat helps to keep it on the doll's head.

The strands of beads are attached underneath the rolled collar.

"Victor. So original. A prize fight on our first date. And I dressed for the opera."

I WAKE UP SCREAMING

Rigadoon

Bead necklaces are strung on flexible threads, so they have a fluid drape to them. They come in an infinite range of colors and bead types. The problem is that the beads all slip off when the thread is cut. The solution is to glue the ends of the thread after cutting it. Then you can apply the string of beads to an outfit, just like prestrung pearls.

Top: The headpiece is a hairband made with strands of beads. One end is sandwiched between a piece of Velcro and a piece of felt. The other is sandwiched between two pieces of Velcro.

Bottom: The ends of the strands are glued to the inside of the dress. The group of strands that hangs free is sandwiched between a button and a piece of Velcro. It attaches to the headpiece.

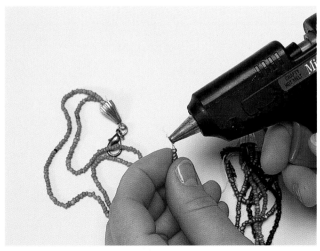

To detach a strand of beads, snip it close to the end. Let a few beads fall off, leaving about 1/2" (1.3cm) of bare string. A bit of glue on the string will prevent the rest of the beads from coming off.

"My itinerary said Caracas, but here I am in Alaska. Dressed to kill. In a cabin. And I'm starving. Hey Charlie, pass me that other boot."

THE GOLD RUSH

Charleston

Fake flowers are another ideal material for doll clothes. The petals are colorful and cheap, they don't need to be hemmed and they come precut in a great variety of interesting shapes. The typical flower has curved petals that hug the doll's figure, so there's no need for extra tailoring.

The hat is made from a few petals glued together at their bottom edges in a fan shape. A loop of elastic is glued underneath. Then it's decorated with feather parts and gilt berries.

Velvet rose petals are a good place to start. Use flowers with fairly big petals. The berries and feathers are for decorating the hat and waistband.

Left: For the hat, start with one petal glued on a loop of elastic. Then glue several more petals in a fan shape around it.

Right: The dress starts with a ribbon waistband. To cover the chest, glue two petals to the center of the waistband. If they are too small to cover the whole chest, glue another tier of petals above them. To make the skirt, glue a row of petals overlapping each other all around the bottom edge of the waistband. Start at the ends of the waistband so that the overlaps fall toward the back. Add a second tier of petals if necessary.

"Alan didn't exactly have the right kind of build for heavy work, but what the heck. We could always use some extra help around the farm. At least I'll have a good reason to get dressed in the morning."

SHANE

Schottische

A petal dress can be made out of small flowers, too. It's the same basic construction method as the Charleston. For the smallest petals, like the pink ones shown here, it helps if you glue several together in a fan shape and then attach the whole group to the dress.

Left: The bouquet is miniature flowers and feather parts glued together with a few strands of prestrung pearls, then wrapped in a couple of flower petals. The wire loop goes around the doll's hand.

Center: The foundation for this gown is a white ribbon waistband with several yellow lace streamers glued around the bottom edge. Start layering on petals from the bottom of the streamers up to the waistband. The bodice is made just like the Charleston, only with more petals to fill it out.

Upper Right: The tiara is made from a loop of prestrung pearls. Cross the ends and hold them in place with a big drop of glue. Then glue the flowers on the front.

"Johnny might not mind swinging around in the same old rag every day, but a girl has just got to get herself all gussied up once in a while."

TARZAN AND HIS MATE

Twist

Feathers can be treated as flower petals. Some feathers even curve naturally to follow the doll's contours. If you need to curve a straight feather, bend the rib against your thumbnail.

This dress starts with a ribbon waistband. The blue feathers are glued around the waistband for the skirt. After gluing on the feathers, you can trim them flush along the bottom edge. Four green feathers are glued in the center to cover the chest.

To decorate the waistband, I peeled some feather parts off the main rib and glued them on.

The doll is holding a feather pom-pom. It starts with a piece of 1/4" (.6cm) wide ribbon glued in a circle, just large enough to fit over the doll's hand. Then fluffy feather parts are glued all around the ribbon.

Left: Feathers are available at craft shops. The fluffy pink and yellow maribou feathers are the most versatile. You can also glean fluff from the bottom of stiff feathers like the green and red ones.
Right: The contributions of pigeons, ducks, geese and seagulls from the local duck pond.
Bottom: Miniature treasures from the local duck pond.

Twist Cape

The cape starts with a choker collar made of 1/4" (.6cm) wide ribbon secured in front with Velcro.

To make the cape part, glue several large feathers along the back of the choker. Then glue feather parts all around.

"How wonderful of Burt to invite me over to the pool. And that pool. And that one over there, too."

THE SWIMMER

Twist Hat

Left: Start with a big magic marker cap. Cover it with felt and glue a loop of elastic inside. Then glue feather fluff around the bottom edge. Top it off with a spray of fluff and a rhinestone.
Bottom Right: To get the fluff, grasp a section of it firmly, close to the main rib, and pull slowly. A thin layer of the rib peels off with the fluff. Let it come—it holds the fluff together. If it doesn't, dot the ends of the fluff with glue before you let go.
Top Right: A section of fluff. It's easier to work with when held together by a layer of rib.

More Feathers

This two-piece outfit is the Saraband camisole and slip covered with maribou feathers. The doll is holding a spray of feathers. A loop of prestrung pearls is glued on so it can slip over her wrist.

Hairband

Center: Start with a hairband made of rickrack secured behind the doll's head with Velcro. Glue feathers along it, with the rib in the center.
Right: Hide the ribs of the feathers under sequins.

Duck and goose feathers, and a bit of lace. The hat is an oval of felt with a feather glued along the front edge. A loop of elastic is glued under the felt.

Pigeon and seagull feathers. The hat is a hairband covered with feathers and a rhinestone earring.

"If I was Farley, I would have taken the bus."

STRANGERS ON A TRAIN

Polka

Clay clothes might sound like a fashion oxymoron, but they're for real. The new polymer modeling clays are widely available at art and craft stores. They come in a startling variety of bright colors, are easy to mold and harden in your oven under moderate heat. All of the glues that I tried made a secure bond between the baked clay, fabric and other materials. The clay comes in small cubes. One cube is more than enough to make a fully accessorized outfit, but I can't resist buying at least two or three at a time to play around with the colors.

This is a three-piece outfit. The clay breastplate is glued to a piece of lace secured in the back with Velcro. The clay apron is made the same way. It's worn over a Cakewalk skirt.

Clay clothes are fairly rugged, but reserve them for display or gentle play.

The apron and breastplate follow the same construction method. First cover the doll's torso with tinfoil. Mold it firmly around her contours, and smooth the wrinkles. Tape the edges so the foil doesn't shift while you're working.

Roll a thin pancake of clay and mold it over the foil. To make the polka dots, dot the pancake with bits of clay in a contrasting color.

Keep the clay to the front of the doll. If you mold it too far around her sides, it won't come off. Also, take into account the position of her limbs. I flared out the bottom of the apron to allow her legs freedom of movement.

When you're satisfied, trim off the excess foil. Gently remove the apron along with the remaining foil underneath. The foil helps the apron keep its shape until it's baked. Follow the manufacturer's instructions for baking. The foil will peel off easily after the clay cools.

"I always knew that Rosie was of two minds. As long as I'm his only girl."
THE THING WITH TWO HEADS

Center: Make a pancake, then mold it on the doll.
Right: After baking, glue the apron on a waistband of lace.

Ballroom

This is a fine-tuned version of the Polka outfit. Instead of a ribbon or lace waistband, the breastplate is glued on a Saraband skirt. It's also glued at the neck to a choker necklace made from a strip of felt secured behind with Velcro.

The mask is glued to a ribbon, secured in back with Velcro. The gauntlets are glued to felt cuffs. For the spear, I used a cheap paintbrush with the bristles trimmed off. The spearhead is molded over one end, removed for baking and then glued back on.

Do not try to bake the clay while it's still on the doll. I tried it. The clay turns out fine, but the doll does not!

"Kenneth probably doesn't do a lot of cooking. I can tell, because he thawed that thing out too soon."

THE THING

Hats

Polymer clay hats. Why not? The Floppy, Spiral, Confetti and Robin Hood hats all start with a round pancake of clay. Instead of molding the hats on the doll's head, mold them on a ball of tinfoil (flatten one side so it doesn't roll around). The ball doesn't have to be exactly the same size as the doll's head. You can also use cones, cubes and pyramids as foundations.

Keep the foil inside the hat while baking. It will come out easily when the clay is cooled. Then glue ribbon, a piece of pipe cleaner or a loop of elastic inside.

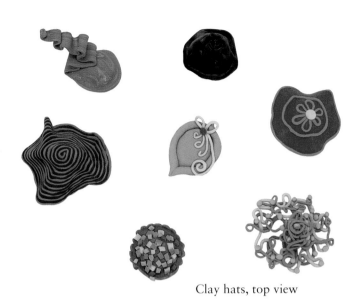

Clay hats, top view

Floppy Hat

Left: Make a foil ball.

Center: Drape a clay pancake over the ball.

Right: Decorate with clay strings and dots. A loop of ribbon is glued underneath.

Spiral Hat

Using two contrasting colors of clay, roll out two long strings, spiral them around each other to make a mat and flatten the mat into a pancake.

Confetti Hat

Cut a zigzag in the edge of a pancake, turn it up to form a brim and sprinkle with clay confetti.

Robin Hood Hat

Turn up the edge of a pancake, roll it over and pinch it on two opposite sides to make the front and back. Decorate with clay strings and dots.

Bag Hat

This hat does not need a foil mold. Make a rectangular pancake about 1¹/₂" (3.8cm) wide, and join the ends to form a tube around the doll's head. Turn up the bottom edge to make a brim. Pinch the top edge closed. Remove from the doll and bake.

Wave Hat

To start the Wave hat, roll out a clay snake and flatten it. The flattened snake should be about 6" (15.2cm) long. One end should come to a point (the tip of the hat), and the other end should be about 1" (2.5cm) wide. Trim the edges evenly. Mold the wide end into a shallow crown with a narrow brim. This makes the main body of the hat. To make the "waves," lay the hat on its side and gently fold the clay back and forth. If you try to do this while the hat is upright, the waves will collapse on each other.

Spaghetti Hat

Make long clay strings, dribble them over a cone-shaped foil base and add clay dots.

Pumps

Pumps follow the same construction method as the sock-boots, without the sock. Since the pumps are molded on the doll's bare feet, they may tend to stick and lose their shape when you remove them. Pull them off gently, then put them back on and lightly press them into shape. It also helps if you put the doll in the fridge for a while (cold clay won't be as sticky as clay that's warmed by your hands).

Fashion doll feet can vary greatly in size. If you're making shoes for a friend, borrow your friend's doll or make sure that your doll has the same-size feet.

When you've finished molding the clay sole for the sock-boot shown in the demonstration here, pull it gently off the sock. It should come away easily. If it loses its shape, lightly press it back on, then take it off again. Bake the clay sole. When it's cool, glue it back on the sock.

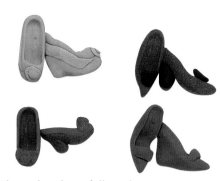

These clay shoes follow the same basic construction method as the Autumn Intrigue sock-boot, without the sock.

Autumn Intrigue Sock-Boot

The sock part is described in chapter two.

1 Make an oval pancake as big as the doll's foot with the sock on.

2 Press the pancake on the sole of the foot. Pinch the toe to a point, and smooth the back up around the heel.

3 **Left:** Start the high heel by making a small cone.
Center: Push the cone over at an angle.
Right: Then press it on the shoe.

Showgirl

Dryer lint helps to make a surprisingly effective modeling compound. To make the modeling compound, collect some lint from your lint trap. Thin some white glue with a little water, then add enough of this mixture to get the lint wet. When the outfit is completed let it air dry. The Showgirl outfit is similar to the Ballroom ensemble except that it uses lint from three loads of laundry.

I wanted to preserve the rough texture, so I added a bit of black paint from my kid's art set to the mixture. Painting the lint after it's dry will smooth out the surface.

The breastplate is glued to a piece of fringe and secured in the back with Velcro. I added a second layer of fringe underneath to fill it out. The shin guards are held at the knee and ankle with loops of elastic. The shield is molded over a plastic soda bottle to give it a curved shape.

Protect the doll's body with a layer of foil. Mold a layer of lint over the foil. Use a fork to rough out the edges, if desired.

"If Kirk thinks he can beat me just 'cause I'm a girl, he can guess again."

SPARTACUS

Vaudeville

Papier-mâché is great for all kinds of fantasy costumes. This outfit is an oversized mask that rests on the doll's shoulders. Her arms are under the yellow skirt. A narrow slit allows her eyes to be seen.

To start the mask, put a cardboard tube over the doll's head. Cut away about 2" (5.1cm) from the bottom front, so the tube rests on the doll's shoulders and extends down her back about an inch. The back extension helps keep the mask steady.

Cut off the top of the tube at an angle. This will give the finished mask a tilt to the front, so it can be seen more easily.

To make the sun part, cut a circle of cardboard from a cereal box. Trim the edge in a zigzag. Wad up some paper and tape it in the center. This will make the sun's face three-dimensional. Then tape the sun on top of the tube.

Cut two arms from cardboard and tape them to the sides of the tube.

The oversized boots are rolled-up newspapers that are bent at one end. The doll's feet do not go into the feet of the boots. They just slip into the leg part.

After you've finished taping the foundation together, cover it with several layers of papier-mâché. Then let it dry, and paint it.

The skirt is part of a doily with extra lace glued on the top and bottom edges. It's glued directly on the papier-mâché tube.

"I told James that I didn't need a makeover. I like myself just the way I am."

VERTIGO

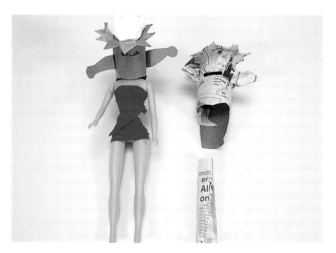

Left and Bottom Right: Make a foundation for the mask and boots from cardboard, tissue and newspaper.
Upper Right: Apply several layers of papier-mâché to the foundation. Let it dry, and then paint it.

Conclusion
To Glue or Not to Glue

If the siren song of needle and thread over-whelms you, just give in. You can sew practically any outfit in this book following the same instructions and substituting stitches for glue.

A sewing machine is not needed. A few hand stitches will hold things together. The results are almost indistinguishable from glue as far as the basic outfits go. The differences show up in the way you choose to embellish them.

Pictured here is a strapless version of the shirt-sleeve gowns from chapter four. This sleeve was generously gathered into a plain cuff. Since I planned for the dress to open in back, I didn't need to preserve the button and buttonhole. I cut them away and just used enough cuff to go around the doll's chest and overlap about 1/2" (1.3cm) in back. The back seam is sewn from the hips down and closed at the waist and top with snaps.

The hat is a small Neshannock hat from chapter four, made from a corner of the shirt collar. It has a piece of wire stitched inside the hem. Both ends of the wire poke out of the back of the hat about 1/2" (1.3cm) like hat pins holding it on the doll's head.

The choker necklace is cut from the shirt's hem. It closes behind the neck with a snap.

After the outfit is completed, stitch on the beads individually. The necklace is sewn to the gown with three loops of beads in front.

You could glue the same basic outfit, only using Velcro instead of snaps. And, as I've shown else-where in this book, you could embellish it by gluing on strings or patches of beads. The result would be different but equally dazzling.

So I would not hem and haw over the question of gluing or sewing. When there's a gal in need of a good dress, be like Cinderella's fairy godmother: Just make it so.

Pogo-
"Steve promised a leisurely driving tour of San Francisco, but, you see, I had a funny feeling about that. I buckled up."

BULLITT